P9-CLN-959

THOMAS WOLFE
A Writer's Life

Thomas Wolfe feeding a chipmunk at the rim of Crater Lake, Oregon, June 20, 1938.

Photo courtesy of the Thomas Wolfe Collection, Pack Memorial Public Library, Asheville, North Carolina.

THOMAS WOLFE
A Writer's Life

Revised Edition

TED MITCHELL

With a Preface by James W. Clark Jr.

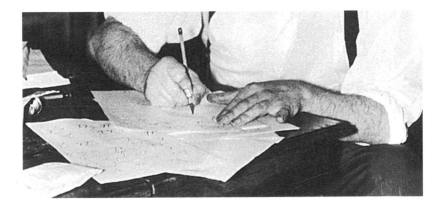

Raleigh
North Carolina Department of Cultural Resources
Division of Archives and History

Published in Cooperation with the
Appalachian Consortium, Boone

LEE COUNTY LIBRARY
107 Hawkins Ave.
Sanford, NC 27330

North Carolina Department of Cultural Resources
Betty Ray McCain, *Secretary*
Elizabeth F. Buford, *Deputy Secretary*

Division of Archives and History
Jeffrey J. Crow, *Director*
Larry G. Misenheimer, *Deputy Director*

North Carolina Historical Commission
William S. Powell (2001), *Chairman*
Alan D. Watson (2003), *Vice-Chairman*

Millie M. Barbee (2003)	Mary Hayes Holmes (2005)	Janet N. Norton(2005)
N. J. Crawford (2001)	H. G. Jones (2001)	Gail W. O'Brian(2005)
T. Harry Gatton (2003)	B. Perry Morrison Jr.(2005)	Max R. Williams (2001)

Appalachian Consortium

Member Institutions

Appalachian State University
Blue Ridge Parkway
Clinch Valley College
East Tennessee State University
Ruth and Billy Graham Children's Health Center
Lees-McRae College
Mars Hill College
Mayland Community College
North Carolina Division of Archives and History
Southern Highlands Craft Guild
Tusculum College
U.S. Forest Service
Warren Wilson College
Western Carolina University

© 1999 by the North Carolina Division of Archives and History
All rights reserved
Revised edition 1999
ISBN 0-86526-286-1

Dedicated to

Aldo P. Magi, in testament to his considerable gifts as a writer, editor, and generous friend to all readers of Thomas Wolfe. The integrity of his work and his dedication to every aspect of Thomas Wolfe's life and literature will always evoke my deep gratitude and admiration.

Contents

Foreword

O FIGURE HOLDS a place more significant in the history of North Carolina literature than the fiction writer Thomas Wolfe of Asheville, North Carolina. An author of tremendous energy, rich imagination, and powerful rhetorical style, he was arguably the first novelist from North Carolina to become a major voice in American literature.

Ted Mitchell's *Thomas Wolfe: A Writer's Life* explores Wolfe's life and career from his birth in the North Carolina mountain community of Asheville in 1900 until his early death in 1938. Mitchell, a historic site interpreter at the Thomas Wolfe Memorial State Historic Site in Asheville, is an expert on Wolfe and has written extensively on his subject. A native of Detroit, Michigan, he was educated at Northwood University in Midland, Michigan, prior to coming to western North Carolina. *Thomas Wolfe: A Writer's Life* also includes a preface by another Wolfe authority, James W. Clark Jr., a professor of English and director of the Humanities Extension/Publications Program at North Carolina

State University and a former president of the Thomas Wolfe Society.

Thomas Wolfe: A Writer's Life originally appeared in an earlier edition published by the Thomas Wolfe Memorial State Historic Site, and the Historical Publications Section gratefully acknowledges that organization's assistance in issuing this second edition, which contains new material by the author. The Historical Publications Section is also pleased to include this title as the second volume in the series on western North Carolina published jointly with the Appalachian Consortium of Boone, North Carolina. In his famous novel *Look Homeward, Angel* and other works, Thomas Wolfe vividly portrayed aspects of life in the mountains of North Carolina in the early twentieth century. By jointly publishing this edition of T*homas Wolfe: A Writer's Life*, the Appalachian Consortium and the Historical Publications Section endeavor to keep that portrait alive for thousands of North Carolinians and visitors to the Old North State.

Joe A. Mobley, Administrator
Historical Publications Section

September 1999

Preface

THOMAS WOLFE of Asheville, North Carolina, wrote extensively about himself, his family, and hundreds of associates in four long novels and a number of short stories. Who has not heard some version of Wolfe's semi-autobiographical performances in work after work? His deliberate manner of developing the legend of himself in fiction is unmistakable. Both Eugene Gant and George Webber, the major characters identifiable as the author, still have currency among readers in this country and abroad. For Wolfe's fiction has been widely translated, and a few of his stories or chapters from the novels appear in classroom anthologies with regularity. More than 80 books about his literary canon have been published. Reviews and critical essays total over a thousand. Both the legend of Thomas Wolfe and some of the characters he created live well in our time.

As an author known for representing much of his own life in fiction, Wolfe also has continued to be of considerable fascination to biographers. Ted Mitchell's account of the Asheville native's life as literary art brings to more than a dozen the number of separate, broadly biographical treatments of this powerful figure who died September 15, 1938, at age 37.

Thomas Wolfe was the youngest child of William Oliver Wolfe, a Pennsylvania stonecutter known as the marble man, and Julia Westall Wolfe, a second-sighted, purse-lipped woman of the North Carolina mountains. Tom never married. His favorite in the family was brother Ben, also a bachelor. The other Wolfe children who lived to adulthood did marry. Effie and Frank produced offspring. Fred and Mabel did not.

Tom was destined to become famous for his romantic yet chastening depictions of his brothers and sisters among the rest. Whether his astonishing memory or his gradually emancipated imagination played the more considerable part in this expanding drama, the fiction writer who had wanted to be a playwright never quite decided himself. Some critics have said that Wolfe was often more conscious of his storytellers than he was of his stories.

His own creative challenges and solutions suggest the artistic predicament of his father. The marble man could not carve an angel acceptable to his own vision. He loved literature and recitation; but his family, his only real audience, was not always appreciative. Still it is clear that W.O. Wolfe's apt memory of literary passages inspired his private performances. Tom remembered Papa's stagecraft. The shrewd mother of the future author used her sharp memory for business matters as an access to real property, most notably city lots and the boardinghouse she purchased in 1906 and operated as the Old Kentucky Home for much of the remainder of her busy life.

Wolfe's own special uses of memory, like his father's and mother's, were powerful and sustained. Not a frustrated private performance, not pieces of private property, Wolfe's memory was proof. And not just page proof. He gave public proof that the dreams of youth are the promises of our lives, our golden weather. There, also, is his abundant proof that we know a face or fact or place or personal pleasure for the first time when we remember it. He teaches us to remember in order to know. He employs memory as proof in the grand, often redundant syntheses of his Gant and Webber materials. This abundance of details comes and returns without apology but with the sure sense that our time-tossed world does have a still center. The swirling swarm of his remembered hometown life, for example, is anchored by a tall granite monument, a core of changelessness in the public square. While we must try to get along together, each of us is a proud, lonely little world.

In 1929 the narrative voice of *Look Homeward, Angel* suggested its long foreground to all readers. Wolfe's notebooks and letters have provided insights and further confirmations since then. During the Depression people in the United States and in England found Wolfe's first book quite hopeful. Readers in the Soviet bloc and Europe later championed the vitalism of its characters. As an experiment in literary modernism, Wolfe's work allowed people involved in complex, simultaneous actions to make sense to readers. In this way his readers undergo an apprenticeship in modern reading as the protagonist Eugene Gant is learning how to live. Gothic techniques and James Joyce's pioneering methods combine in Eugene's mind with classical learning and popular culture from his crib to college. In Wolfe the streams of consciousness run clear.

Yet voracious everyday living is life to Wolfe. Appetite may seem at times to be all there is. His patron and mistress Aline Bernstein; Maxwell Perkins, the Scribner's editor who loved Wolfe as a son—sternly and dearly; and the redoubtable literary agent Elizabeth Nowell who could also edit: all tasted his bittersweet success and failure. Others of equal literary power and influence did not appreciate his work or champion it, however.

Of Time and the River came out in March 1935 as some critics expressed the opinion that Wolfe was a one-book writer. He had had his own doubts—plus worry and depression. But his material and his associates sustained him. Travel, especially travel in Germany, bolstered him too. His early and lifelong love of trains enlarged to embrace ocean liners. On the *Olympic* in August 1925 he first met Mrs. Bernstein. Employed by Wolfe from 1933 until his death in 1938, Miss Nowell became his first important biographer in 1960 after editing a volume of his letters. She was especially incisive in presenting him in the whirl of literary New York and the frenzy of his creative binges and hangovers. Max Perkins was Wolfe's designated executor and estate trustee, always his conservator.

This famous editor was not the person who put Wolfe's posthumous novels into shape and into print, however. Those controversial tasks fell to Edward Aswell of Harper and Brothers. Wolfe had begun to work with Aswell in 1937–1938. *The Web and the Rock* (1939) and *You Can't Go Home Again* (1940) have led a continuing line of new titles by Wolfe, some published as recently as the 1990s. His short fiction has been issued in a standard edition by Scribner's, and several of his plays are now in print. The *Thomas Wolfe Review* is published semiannually by the Thomas Wolfe Society, an international organization with a broad membership. In Asheville an annual festival is held each fall in honor and memory of the sensitive local boy whose home, his mother's boardinghouse, is now a North Carolina state historic site. Collections of Wolfe materials are in private hands as well as in Asheville archives and the valuable holdings of Wolfe's two alma maters. Since their separate publications, his major books have never been out of print. Foreign language editions are available today in Europe and Asia.

As a native of western North Carolina with an absorbing interest in himself and language as well as the South, Thomas Wolfe spent much of his adult life elsewhere, New York and Europe in particular. For seven years after he became a literary personality, he did not come back to Asheville at all. His career can actually be characterized by his longing for home and his perplexing avoidance of home. Perhaps it was not avoidance, though. Look as he might, he could not find his true home standing anywhere on the earth for him to enter and settle down. His far wandering is represented and celebrated in his writing, his true abode. His protagonists Eugene Gant and George Webber provide his enduring proofs in their separate and different enactments of Wolfe's vaunted memory and increasingly agile imagination. Long live Thomas Wolfe's storyland.

James W. Clark Jr.

1

Asheville
1900 – 1916

Born to Mr. & Mrs. W. O. Wolfe, a son.
—Asheville Daily Citizen

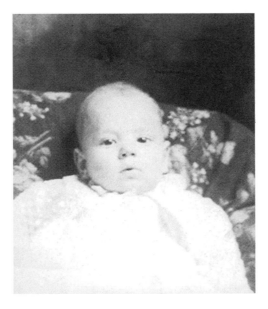

Thomas Clayton Wolfe, four months old. ". . . the tiny acorn from which the mighty oak must grow, the heir of all the ages, the inheritor of unfulfilled renown . . ." (*Look Homeward, Angel*, 34.)

Photo courtesy of The North Carolina Collection, University of North Carolina Library at Chapel Hill, and the Estate of Thomas Wolfe.

THOMAS CLAYTON WOLFE was born on October 3, 1900, at 92 Woodfin Street, Asheville, North Carolina, the last of W.O. and Julia Wolfe's eight children. Although his name did not appear in print when the *Daily Citizen* routinely reported the event, he was named Thomas after his maternal grandfather, Thomas Casey Westall, and great-great-grandfather, Thomas Westall. He received his middle name, Clayton, from a spiritualist clergyman, William Clayton Bowman, whom his mother admired. His father descended from hardy Pennsylvania German-Dutch-English farmers; his mother

Thomas Wolfe's "Altamont"—Asheville, North Carolina—as it appeared in 1902 when he was a child. "I think no one could understand Thomas Wolfe who had not seen or properly imagined the place in which he was born and grew up," Wolfe's editor, Maxwell Perkins, wrote in 1947. "Asheville, North Carolina, is encircled by mountains. The trains wind in and out through labyrinths of passes. A boy of Wolfe's imagination imprisoned there could think that what was beyond was all wonderful—different from what it was where there was not for him enough of anything." (*Harvard Library Bulletin*, Autumn 1947: 275–276.)

Photo courtesy of The North Carolina Collection, Pack Memorial Public Library, Asheville, North Carolina.

was a third-generation North Carolinian of Scots-Irish-English stock. Thomas Wolfe was proud to claim that "One half of me is great fields and mighty barns, and one half of me is the great hills of North Carolina."[1]

Wolfe's father, William Oliver Wolfe, was born on his father's farm in Adams County, Pennsylvania, on April 10, 1851. Although his gravestone at Asheville's Riverside Cemetery reads "BORN AT GETTYSBURG PA," he was born in rural Latimore Township, three miles from York Springs and 17 miles northeast of Gettysburg. He was the seventh of Jacob and Eleanor Jane (Heikes) Wolf's nine children. His father died when W.O. was nine, and his mother struggled with the Herculean hardships of maintaining the family farm.

As there were already several stonecutters in the Wolf and Heikes families, W.O. was persuaded by his mother after the Civil War to become a stonecutter. At 15 he apprenticed himself to Hugh and Martin A. Sisson, who ran a stonecutting shop in

William Oliver Wolfe, age 24. Thomas Wolfe's father was familiarly known as "W.O." and depicted fictionally as "W.O. Gant" in *Look Homeward, Angel* and *Of Time and the River.*

Photo courtesy of The North Carolina Collection, University of North Carolina Library at Chapel Hill, and the Estate of Thomas Wolfe.

Baltimore. In the evenings W.O. delighted in the plays of Shake-speare. At a height of 6'4" and possessing an oratorical booming voice, he could well have become an actor. Over the years he be-came a highly skilled artisan, as several existing examples of marble doorstops and paperweights he carved for family mem-bers attest. He could carve "The dove, the lamb, the smooth joined marble hands of death, and letters fair and fine—but not the angel."[2] In *Look Homeward, Angel* Thomas Wolfe used the simpering marble angel from Carrara to symbolize his father's frustrated dreams and ambitions.

While still a teenager, W.O. learned of job openings in the South. In 1869 he was hired to trim the South Carolina state capitol in Columbia that had been damaged during the Civil War. By 1870 he had moved to North Carolina to work on con-structing the state penitentiary in Raleigh. He quickly prospered and entered into a partnership with John Cayton as a marble cutter in a shop on the corner of South Blount and East Morgan Streets. During these happy days of prosperity and success, W.O. added the "e" to his last name for a more elegant "Wolfe." His halcyon days ended on October 9, 1873, when he married Hattie J. Watson, marking the first of three troubled marriages. Al-though the couple separated less than 15 months later, the di-vorce suit was not settled until 1876. Both charged sexual incompatibility and filed for annulments, claiming their mar-riage had never been consummated.

On March 25, 1879, W.O. married the tubercular spinster Cynthia C. Hill, eight years his senior. Later that year he ar-ranged a move to Asheville, a mountain community well known for its treatment of tuberculars. Cynthia went ahead to Asheville and opened a millinery shop on College Street, and ironically, Julia Westall was Cynthia's first customer. W.O. closed his Raleigh shop and joined Cynthia in Asheville. His second mar-riage lasted less than five years: Cynthia died of tuberculosis on February 22, 1884, in the house W.O. had built for her at 92 Woodfin Street.

Hattie J. Watson, the first of W.O. Wolfe's three wives. In divorce proceedings she charged W.O. with impotence and "brutal violence," both verbal and physical. W.O.'s violence established a pattern that would repeat itself during his marriages to Cynthia Hill and Julia Westall.

Photo courtesy of The North Carolina Collection, University of North Carolina Library at Chapel Hill, and the Estate of Thomas Wolfe.

Cynthia C. Hill, W.O. Wolfe's second wife, "a gaunt tubercular spinstress, ten years his elder, but with a nest egg and an unshakable will to matrimony." (*Look Homeward, Angel,* 5.) Cynthia was actually only eight years older than W.O.

Photo courtesy of the North Carolina Department of Cultural Resources.

Despite his alcoholism, W.O. Wolfe was a hard worker and a good provider for his family. By the time he married Julia Westall on January 14, 1885, he had already established a successful monument shop on the edge of Asheville's public square. Thomas Wolfe admired the fact that his father was largely a self-educated man. Along with the broad rhetoric he affected, W.O. could recite soliloquies from Shakespeare, as well as the poetry of Gray and Poe.

Julia Elizabeth Westall was born on February 16, 1860, in Swannanoa, nine miles east of Asheville. Her ancestor, Peter Penland, had been a captain under George Washington during the French and Indian War; Thomas Wolfe's great-great-great-aunt, Elizabeth Patton, a Swannanoa native, was the second wife of frontiersman Davy Crockett. Julia was born a year before the Civil War began and grew up on her father's farm during the hard years of Reconstruction. She was but one of Thomas Casey and Martha Penland Westall's 11 children. Julia's grasping and parsimonious nature was greatly influenced by the deprivations she shared with her family on the Westall farm in Swannanoa. "The poverty and privation of these years had been so terrible that none of them ever spoke of it now," Thomas Wolfe recorded in *Look Homeward, Angel*, "but the bitter steel had sheared into their hearts, leaving scars that would not heal."[3]

Although Julia's childhood was spent in near poverty, she managed to enjoy mountain pastimes: she played the violin,

Julia Westall Wolfe in 1882 during her teaching days in the western North Carolina mountains. Thomas Wolfe's mother was depicted fictionally as "Eliza Gant" in *Look Homeward, Angel* and *Of Time and the River*.

Photo courtesy of The North Carolina Collection, University of North Carolina Library at Chapel Hill, and the Estate of Thomas Wolfe.

attended church, hymn sings, country dances, and quiltings. She was such an excellent marksman with a rifle that she later claimed "the boys didn't want to shoot with me when I was a girl."[4] She attended a one-room school in Swannanoa for four years and then did not go to school again for eight years. Although Julia acquired only two more years of formal education at the Asheville Female Seminary and Judson College in Hendersonville (both really high schools), she bluffed her way into jobs as a country school teacher and began saving her wages to buy property. Real estate speculation would soon rule her life. A shrewd, tough woman of slightly less than middle height (5'4"), her impoverished youth would provide her with independence and fierce determination. She supplemented her teaching income by becoming a book agent, taking orders from door to door, sometimes riding from town to town on horseback.

On October 18, 1884, Julia entered W.O. Wolfe's monument shop and met the recently widowed tombstone maker for the first time. Julia was looking for a prospective customer rather

W.O. Wolfe's monument shop at 22 South Pack Square—"a two-story shack of brick, with wide wooden steps, leading down to the square from a marble porch." (*Look Homeward, Angel,* 17.)
Photo courtesy of the North Carolina Department of Cultural Resources.

than a husband, but W.O. fell in love with her at first sight, and they were married three months later. At their first meeting she solicited a Civil War novel, *Thorns in the Flesh*—a title that proved all too prophetic for the couple's turbulent marriage. Julia's marriage was slated for unhappiness from the beginning. When W.O. proposed to her, she was still in love with young Mark Lance, although she had long ago stopped seeing him. She told W.O. that she would never love another man as she had once loved Lance, but that did not discourage W.O. from marrying her.

Julia Wolfe was an enterprising and resourceful woman who worked hard to improve her family's economic position. She never quite approved of her husband's vocation as a tombstone maker: people, she felt, did not die fast enough. Becoming a wife and mother did not curtail her industry. She stopped teaching, but began accepting boarders at the Woodfin Street house and became even more obsessed with wheeling and dealing in the real estate market of the growing resort town. By the time of Thomas Wolfe's birth, Julia was "almost never at home" and all but "completely absorbed in her real estate speculations."[5]

Thomas Wolfe lived the first six years of his life at 92 Woodfin Street, the frame and plaster house his father had built for Cynthia in October 1881. Julia later complained she was getting both a secondhand house and a secondhand husband. Woodfin Street was the birthplace for all eight of W.O. and Julia's children:

1. Leslie E. Wolfe ("Leslie" in *Look Homeward, Angel*)
2. Effie Nelson Wolfe Gambrell ("Daisy Gant Gambell")
3. Frank Cecil Wolfe ("Steve Gant")
4. Mabel Elizabeth Wolfe Wheaton ("Helen Gant Barton")
5. Benjamin Harrison Wolfe ("Benjamin Harrison Gant")
6. Grover Cleveland Wolfe ("Grover Cleveland Gant")
7. Frederick William Wolfe ("Luke Gant")
8. Thomas Clayton Wolfe ("Eugene Gant" in *Look Homeward, Angel* and *Of Time and the River;* and "George Webber" in *The Web and the Rock* and *You Can't Go Home Again*)

Thomas Wolfe's birthplace, 92 Woodfin Street, Asheville, July 4, 1899. Pictured left to right: unidentified servant, Effie, Mabel, Frank, Grover, Fred, Ben, W.O., and Julia Wolfe.

Photo courtesy of The North Carolina Collection, University of North Carolina Library at Chapel Hill, and the Estate of Thomas Wolfe.

Julia Wolfe with Leslie, the first of her eight children. Leslie died of infant cholera at the age of nine months. "I thought the end of the world had come when Leslie died," Mrs. Wolfe later stated. (*The Marble Man's Wife*, 44.)

Photo courtesy of The North Carolina Collection, University of North Carolina Library at Chapel Hill, and the Estate of Thomas Wolfe.

"... the maidenly Daisy," Effie Nelson Wolfe Gambrell. "She was a timid, sensitive girl ... industrious and thorough in her studies. ... She had very little fire, or denial in her. ..." (*Look Homeward, Angel,* 45.)

Photo courtesy of The Thomas Wolfe Collection, Pack Memorial Public Library, Asheville, North Carolina.

Frank Cecil Wolfe, W.O. and Julia's third child and the eldest of the five Wolfe brothers.

Photo courtesy of The Thomas Wolfe Collection, Park Memorial Public Library, Asheville, North Carolina.

Mabel Elizabeth Wolfe Wheaton. "She has more human greatness in her than any woman I've ever known," Thomas Wolfe wrote of his sister in 1925. (*Letters,* 80.)

Photo courtesy of The North Carolina Collection, University of North Carolina Library at Chapel Hill, and the Estate of Thomas Wolfe.

Benjamin Harrison Wolfe. Thomas Wolfe stated that "the Asheville I knew died for me when Ben died. . . . I think that his death affected me more than any other event in my life." (*Letters*, 178.)

Photo courtesy of The North Carolina Collection, University of North Carolina Library at Chapel Hill, and the Estate of Thomas Wolfe.

Grover Cleveland Wolfe, 1903. "This was Grover—the gentlest and saddest of the boys." (*Look Homeward, Angel*, 55.)

Photo courtesy of The Thomas Wolfe Collection, Pack Memorial Public Library, Asheville, North Carolina.

Frederick William Wolfe—"he was Luke, the unique, Luke, the incomparable: he was, in spite of his garrulous and fidgeting nervousness, an intensely likable person—and he really had in him a bottomless well of affection." (*Look Homeward, Angel*, 121.)

Photo courtesy of The North Carolina Collection, University of North Carolina Library at Chapel Hill, and the Estate of Thomas Wolfe.

"Tom," ca. 1907.

Photo courtesy of The North Carolina Collection, University of North Carolina Library at Chapel Hill, and the Estate of Thomas Wolfe.

A complacent and silent infant, Thomas Wolfe later reported "Moo" was his "First articulate speech."[6] W.O. had carried him into the orchard behind the family home and Tom had begun imitating the sound of a cow near a neighbor's fence. "He can talk," W.O. boasted to Julia, "he said Moo."[7] The proud father told the story over and over, getting Tom to repeat the sound for every visitor to the house that day. The infant grew into an adult with splendid recall. "I have tried to make myself conscious of the whole of my life since first the baby in the basket became conscious of the warm sunlight on the porch," he later wrote, "and saw his sister go up the hill to the girl's school on the corner (the first thing I remember)."[8] He recalled the Hazzard's great house on the hill to the east of the family home and the day that his head was almost crushed by a horse pulling a grocery wagon. Although he was not seriously injured in the accident, he always bore a small scar on his forehead he called "the mark of the centaur."[9]

In April 1904 Wolfe traveled with his mother, sister Mabel, and brothers Fred, Ben, and Grover to St. Louis. Planning to mix business with pleasure, Julia rented a large house at 5095 Fairmount Avenue to operate as a boardinghouse for visitors from Asheville to the World's Fair. She called it "The North Carolina." The oldest children, Frank and Effie, remained in Asheville with their father (although Frank soon joined Julia and the other children). Another motive of Julia's for going to St. Louis was to remove herself and the children from W.O.'s increasing outbursts and alcoholic rampages. Like her fictional counterpart, "Eliza," Julia's "enormous patience was wearing very thin because of the daily cycle of abuse."[10] Once settled in St. Louis, Grover and Fred were sent to work at the Inside Inn, a hotel built for the fair. Julia's venture was cut short on November 16 when Grover died of typhoid fever contracted while working at the fairgrounds. The family immediately returned to Asheville, where Julia was disconsolate and could not help blaming herself for taking the family to St. Louis.

Julia's hopes had actually been fastened on Grover, whom she considered the brightest of her children, rather than Tom, but after Grover's death, she grew more and more possessive of the last of her eight children. By now Tom had already experienced an unusually prolonged infantile relationship with his mother. He nursed until he was three-and-a-half. He slept in the same bed with her until he was nine and older. His Little Lord Fauntleroy curls, stylish at the turn of the century, but usually shorn when a boy entered school, were not cut until Tom was

Thomas Wolfe with second cousin Mary Louise Wolfe, New Orleans, February 24, 1909. Julia Wolfe kept Tom in curls until he was nine, wanting to keep him her baby as long as possible. A few days before he died in 1938, as he lay on a hospital bed at Johns Hopkins Hospital, Julia kissed him on the forehead and reminded him, "You're my baby." And even five years after his death, Julia told an interviewer, "Tom will always be my.baby; he will never seem grown up to me."

Photo courtesy of The Thomas Wolfe Collection, Pack Memorial Public Library, Asheville, North Carolina.

nine. The curls symbolized Tom's childhood, which Julia would never be willing to relinquish. In *Look Homeward, Angel* Wolfe described the "agony and humiliation"[11] his curls cost him. Only after he contracted head lice from one of the neighborhood boys, did his mother relent and allow his curls to be clipped.

On August 30, 1906, hoping to cash in on Asheville's tourist trade, Julia purchased a boardinghouse called Old Kentucky Home at 48 Spruce Street. Only two blocks from the family home, the "dirty yellow"[12] Queen Anne house was comprised of 18 rooms. (Ten years later Julia would add 11 more.) The house was built in 1883 by prominent Asheville banker Erwin E. Sluder, and by 1906 a "malign influence"[13] pervaded the rooms and halls. In *Look Homeward, Angel* Wolfe described "the bleak horror of Dixieland"[14] and claimed the house possessed "All the comforts of the Modern Jail."[15]

Old Kentucky Home ("Dixieland" in *Look Homeward, Angel*), 48 Spruce Street, Asheville. Julia Wolfe purchased the boardinghouse from retired minister Reverend T. M. Myers, who gave the house its name in honor of his home state.

Photo courtesy of The North Carolina Collection, University of North Carolina Library at Chapel Hill, and the Estate of Thomas Wolfe.

As noted, Julia had accepted boarders at 92 Woodfin Street to supplement the family's income while the children were growing up. Despite Grover's death, Julia's St. Louis venture had been profitable, and now she hoped the Old Kentucky Home would prove to be the money-maker she envisioned. She took only six-year-old Tom with her when she moved into the boardinghouse that fall. Her other children remained with their father at the family home, with both Effie and Mabel sharing household duties until they married. Julia's need for money came first: "When she bought this boardinghouse in [1906], she more or less left us," Tom's sister Mabel later explained. "She was busy with her boarders."[16]

Deprived of privacy and security, the move into the Old Kentucky Home began a bewildering new era of Thomas Wolfe's life. Although he often shared a bedroom with Julia, he was, more often than not, shuffled "from room to little room"[17] wherever there was space, to make room for his mother's paying guests. And not only was he moved at random, but when the Old Kentucky Home filled with summer tourists, he was sent back to the Woodfin Street house. He later described himself as "a vagabond since I was seven—with two roofs and no home."[18]

Although family life began to disintegrate after his removal to the boardinghouse, Wolfe experienced a release from his dismal existence when he entered Orange Street School in 1906. He would attend the elementary school from 1906 to 1912, the first to sixth grades. Although he was too young for the city's regulation age of six to begin school, when he tagged along one day with his neighbor Max Israel, his teacher, Elizabeth Bernard, allowed him to stay.[19]

Despite "the misery, drunkenness, and disorder"[20] within the Wolfe households, Tom's childhood was not an altogether unhappy one. The backyard at 92 Woodfin Street with the playhouse W.O. had built for the children was a veritable paradise of cherry, plum, and apple trees. The family home reverberated with noise and laughter, dominated for the most part by W.O.'s earthy humor and rhetoric. Tom long remembered the roaring fires his father built in the parlor and how at the dinner table W.O. heaped Tom's plate with food. He enjoyed visiting his father's monument shop, admiring the haunting marble angels on the porch, and obtaining change from his father to purchase treats. Tom loved reading, curling up on the lounge in the parlor of the family home, or sequestering himself in the privacy of the playhouse to read book after book. W.O. often took Tom to the movies on the square or to Riverside Park for the amusements, but Tom's most gratifying pastime was to bury himself in the books at the public library after school—reading more books, the librarian claimed, than any boy in North Carolina.

Tom also journeyed throughout the South on trips with his mother. Julia usually leased the boardinghouse during the winter months and made several trips out of state for her health, real estate speculation, or for Tom to see something of the country. From 1907 to 1916, mother and son traveled to Florida (St. Petersburg, Jacksonville, St. Augustine, Daytona Beach, Palm Beach), New Orleans, Hot Springs, and—in 1913—to Washington, D.C., to attend the first inauguration of Woodrow Wilson. As usual Tom was treated as an infant, having to share a room with his mother, as well as witness her constant parsimony. Tom later described meals made from leftovers Julia had taken from restaurants: "Humiliation over her stinginess—the incessant wrangling—and the rolls and bread in the bedroom."[21]

In 1911 John Munsey Roberts became principal of Orange Street School. To compare progress of students from grade to grade as well as recruit students for a private school for boys he and his wife were planning to establish soon, Mr. Roberts held a writing competition. Because his wife, Margaret, had never heard of any of the students, Mr. Roberts took the papers home and asked her to help him select the best one, knowing her judgment would be unprejudiced. After reading 60 or more papers, she suddenly came to Tom Wolfe's. Looking up, she declared to her husband, "This boy, Tom Wolfe, is a genius! And I want him for our school next year."[22] This marked the first time anyone referred to Wolfe as a genius. After more than a little persuading by Mr. Roberts, W.O. agreed to pay the tuition of $100 a year, and Thomas Wolfe became the first student enrolled in the North State Fitting School. He later described his four years (1912–1916) at the Robertses' school as "the happiest and most valuable years of my life."[23]

Biographer Andrew Turnbull aptly described Margaret Roberts as "the fairy godmother of Tom's

Margaret Hines Roberts in 1901 at the age of 25.
Photo courtesy of Margaret Rose Roberts.

youth."[24] A major influence upon Wolfe's life, Mrs. Roberts nurtured his talent as a writer and awakened in him a love for fine literature. He had read indiscriminately before meeting Mrs. Roberts, but, as he later stated, "It was through her that I first developed a taste for good literature which opened up a shining El Dorado for me."[25] Because of Mrs. Roberts's affection and compassion for the young, awkward Wolfe, she became the invincible mentor he called the "mother of my spirit."[26]

In an emotion-charged letter written to Mrs. Roberts in 1927 while he was writing *Look Homeward, Angel*, Wolfe revealed his feelings about his teacher:

> I was without a home—a vagabond since I was seven—with two roofs and no home. I moved inward on that house of death and tumult from room to little room, as the boarders came with their dollar a day, and their constant rocking on the

porch. My overloaded heart was bursting with its packed weight of loneliness and terror; I was strangling, without speech, without articulation, in my own secretions—groping like a blind sea-thing with no eyes and a thousand feelers toward light, toward life, toward beauty and order, out of that hell of chaos, greed, and cheap ugliness—and then found you, when else I should have died, you mother of my spirit who fed me with light.[27]

In 1914, while attending the Robertses' school, Wolfe took a paper route for the *Asheville Citizen*. Although his studies were demanding, his parents wanted him to learn the value of money. From his 14th to 16th year, he rose from his bed at four in the morning to deliver newspapers, finishing his route only in time to have breakfast before going to school. His body craved sleep, but he loved the wonder of the dawn breaking upon Asheville's surrounding hills. At school he continued to read omnivorously and, despite his tendency to stammer, he excelled in debate (because of his tenacity, his team always won). During his four years at North State School, he received instruction in Latin, Greek, English, history, mathematics, and German. However, it was his study of literature with Mrs. Roberts that he loved best. Mrs. Roberts guided him through *The Cloister and the Hearth*, *A Midsummer Night's Dream*, *Henry V*, *King Lear*, the Romantic poets, and—among numerous other books—the Old Testament.

On May 13, 1916, North State School participated in the Shakespearean pageant commemorating the tercentenary of Shakespeare's death. "I [*was*] Prince Hal," Wolfe recorded in *The Autobiographical Outline*, "the tights from Philadelphia—four inches too short. . . ."[28] J.M. Roberts's sister, Emma, a math teacher at the school, substituted the remnants of a clown costume for the inadequate tights. The audience roared with laughter at the sight of Wolfe's preposterous appearance and the sensitive, self-conscious boy was slow to recover from his humiliation.

A month before the end of Wolfe's four years at the Robertses' school, he won the bronze medal of the *Independent Magazine*'s citywide school essay contest celebrating the tercentenary with "Shakespeare: the Man." Wolfe tore the Chandos portrait of the bard from the newspaper announcing the contest and nailed it to the wall, scrawling below it, "My Shakespeare, rise!" Mrs. Roberts persuaded Tom to recast "Shakespeare: the Man" in oratorical form for the student declamation contest, which he also won. On June 1, 1916, Wolfe graduated from North State School with several awards, but not with the highest honors. "In other than literary works, other boys with fine minds and regular habits of study far surpassed Tom in the classroom," Mrs. Roberts later wrote. "We knew that this was not because he could not learn those subjects; they simply did not fire him."[29]

At the end of the summer, Wolfe and his family engaged in a heated debate over where he was to go to college. Tom preferred the University of Virginia or Princeton, but his father insisted on the state university at Chapel Hill. W.O. believed the University of North Carolina would prove valuable for connections that would be important for the career in law and politics he envisioned for his son. "You're a North Carolinian and you'll go to North Carolina," W.O. told Tom. "Go to work if you don't go to North Carolina."[30] Tom grudgingly accepted his father's dictum, and on September 10, 1916, expressed his disappointment to his brother-in-law Ralph Wheaton:

> I arrived at my decision to attend our state university last Wednesday night. Perhaps I should say *forced* instead of arrived. For that was what it amounted to. For I had held out for the University of Virginia in spite of the family's protests. But when no reply came from the University of Virginia, I consented to go to Carolina. Two days later a letter did come from Virginia telling me to come on. However, it was too late. But, nevertheless, Carolina is a good school, and perhaps everything is for the best.[31]

NOTES

1. *The Letters of Thomas Wolfe to His Mother*, C. Hugh Holman and Sue Fields Ross, eds. (Chapel Hill: University of North Carolina Press, 1968), 162.

2. Thomas Wolfe, *Look Homeward, Angel* (New York: Charles Scribner's Sons, 1929), 4–5.

3. *Ibid.*, 13–14.

4. R. Dietz Wolfe, M.D., "The 'Gants' Remembered," *Thomas Wolfe Review* 7:1 (Spring 1983): 29.

5. Elaine Westall Gould, *Look Behind You, Thomas Wolfe* (Hicksville, NY: Exposition Press, 1976), 34.

6. Thomas Wolfe, *The Autobiographical Outline for* Look Homeward, Angel, Lucy Conniff and Richard S. Kennedy, eds. (Thomas Wolfe Society, 1991), 4.

7. Richard Walser, "The McCoy Papers," *Thomas Wolfe Review* 5:1 (Spring 1981): 4.

8. *The Letters of Thomas Wolfe to His Mother*, 43.

9. *Look Homeward, Angel*, 44.

10. *Ibid.*, 48.

11. *Ibid.*, 89.

12. *Ibid.*, 127. Exterior paint research of the Old Kentucky Home in 1997 revealed that the house was once painted a dull, medium yellow.

13. *Ibid.*, 128.

14. *Ibid.*, 217.

15. *Ibid.*, 225.

16. Lou Harshaw, *Asheville: Places of Discovery* (Asheville, NC: Bright Mountain Books, 1980), 118. Note: In this interview, Mabel incorrectly gives the date of the purchase of the Old Kentucky Home as 1907.

17. *Look Homeward, Angel*, 137.

18. *The Letters of Thomas Wolfe*, Elizabeth Nowell, ed. (New York: Charles Scribner's Sons, 1956), 123.

19. Julia Wolfe and Elizabeth Bernard claimed that Wolfe was five-and-a-half when he started school; Wolfe's sister Mabel claimed he was five years, five months. Although September 1906 is most certainly when Wolfe formally began the first grade, it is possible he began school informally five or six months earlier, tagging along with Max Israel.

20. *Look Homeward, Angel*, 225.

21. *The Autobiographical Outline*, 8.

22. Margaret Rose Roberts to Ted Mitchell, ALS, 7 pp., April 16, 1995.

23. David Herbert Donald, *Look Homeward: A Life of Thomas Wolfe* (Boston: Little, Brown and Company, 1987), 25.

24. Andrew Turnbull, *Thomas Wolfe* (New York: Charles Scribner's Sons, 1967), 13.

25. *The Letters of Thomas Wolfe to His Mother*, 23.

26. *Letters*, 123. Mrs. Roberts was portrayed as "Margaret Leonard" in *Look Homeward, Angel.*

27. *Ibid.*, 123.

28. *The Autobiographical Outline*, 27.

29. Margaret Roberts, "'An Uncommon Urchin,' Thomas Wolfe: A Memoir—I," *Thomas Wolfe Review* 14:1 (Spring 1990): 12.

30. Richard Walser, *Thomas Wolfe Undergraduate* (Durham, NC: Duke University Press, 1977), 5.

31. *Letters*, 2–3.

2

Chapel Hill
1916 – 1920

*By God, I shall spend the rest of my life getting my
heart back, healing and forgetting every scar you
put upon me when I was a child. The first move I
ever made, after the cradle, was to crawl for the
door, and every move I have made since has been
an effort to escape.*

—*Look Homeward, Angel*, 505

Thomas Wolfe, age 16.
Photo courtesy of the North Carolina Department
of Cultural Resources.

D RESSED neatly in a Biltmore homespun suit, Thomas Wolfe boarded the early morning train for Durham and then, by auto, his final destination of Chapel Hill. By train he finally escaped his tumultuous family; his love for trains and journeying to new places never abated. He was three weeks short of his 16th birthday and already 6'3" tall when he arrived at the University of North Carolina on September 12, 1916, the first day of registration.

Despite the fact that his father was paying the bills and planned a career in law for him, Wolfe decided to continue the literary studies he had begun at the North State School. Besides Greek, Latin, and English, he enrolled in required courses of algebra and trigonometry. On September 23 he reported to the Dialectic Literary Society to seek membership. Housed in Old West Hall, the Di, as it was known, trained students in debate and public speaking. The walls of the third-floor hall where the society was located were lined with portraits of former members who had achieved fame in the history of North Carolina (such as statesman and Civil War governor Zebulon Vance). The ritual of initiation required new members to speak before the audience. A week after his embarrassing initiation into the Di, Wolfe wrote his brother Fred:

> I was the first called on. The society hall is lined with the pictures of the distinguished men once belonging to this society. The portrait of Zeb Vance hangs right over the rostrum. In my little talk I told 'em I was both happy and proud to be in such distinguished company. I ended by telling 'em I hoped they would have the pleasure some day of seeing my picture hang beside Zeb Vance's.[1]

Although Di Society members laughed at this naive pronouncement, Thomas Wolfe's portrait hangs in the Di hall today.

"He belonged, perhaps, to an older and simpler race of men: he belonged with the Mythmakers," Wolfe brashly proclaimed in *Look Homeward, Angel.* "For him, the sun was a lordly lamp to light him on his grand adventuring. . . . He exulted in his

Thomas Wolfe's favorite freshman course was Greek, taught by William Stanly "Bully" Bernard ("Edward Pettigrew 'Buck' Benson" in *The Web and the Rock*). A particularly demanding instructor, Bernard led Wolfe through Homer, Plato, and Euripedes and instilled in Wolfe a love for Greek culture and philosophy. The study of ancient Greek under Bernard greatly influenced Wolfe's first two novels in which he made extensive use of Greek philosophy and myth.

Photo courtesy of The North Carolina Collection, University of North Carolina Library at Chapel Hill.

youth, and he believed that he could never die."[2] But his first year at Chapel Hill was also filled with loneliness and pain. Besides the humiliating Di speech, within his first few weeks at the campus, he was made the dupe of several jokes. He listened attentively to a sermon in chapel by a sophomore with a fake beard. He prepared studiously for an examination on the contents of the college catalogue. "He was conspicuous at once not only because of his blunders," he recorded in *Look Homeward, Angel*, "but also because of his young wild child's face, and his great raw length of body, with the bounding scissor legs."[3] Regardless of his painful self-consciousness, Wolfe was quick to move into the mainstream of campus activity. He helped organize the Freshman Debating Club, mixed with upperclassmen on an equal basis, and despite his literary portrait of the introverted freshman Eugene Gant, was quite gregarious on campus.

The university library contained 75,000 volumes, and Wolfe loaded his arms with books (whether they were required reading or not) and spent much of his free time reading in his room. He also tried out for the track team but eventually gave up; his participation in athletics was confined to horseshoe pitching and baseball catching. He eagerly attended smokers and bull sessions with his fellow students, and in the spring of 1917, as the United States entered World War I, he drilled for military training five evenings a week.

When Wolfe returned home at the end of his freshman year, he was more determined than ever to leave Chapel Hill, despite the intellectual nourishment he had received there. He now wished to continue his education at Princeton. Although he corresponded with the registrar at Princeton, at the end of the summer his father told him that he would have to return to the University of North Carolina or give up his studies altogether.

The summer of 1917 was, for the most part, an ambiguous one for Wolfe. Once home, he was expected to go to work. He was paid $15 a week as Ralph Wheaton's office boy in the Asheville office of the National Cash Register Company. The stress of the war affected nearly everything and everyone. His brother Fred had enlisted in the navy, while his brother Ben had been rejected for the draft because of his weak lungs. Mabel had married the previous year and had moved to Raleigh, but she had returned with her husband, Ralph Wheaton, to 92 Woodfin Street, where she cared for her slowly dying father.

Although Wolfe was promiscuous that summer with women of dubious virtue boarding at the Old Kentucky Home, he fell hopelessly in love with one of his mother's summer boarders, Clara Paul, from Washington, North Carolina. Portrayed as "Laura James" in *Look Homeward, Angel*, Clara was five years older than Wolfe, and his desperate love for her was one-sided. Accompanied by her 11-year-old brother, Ray, who was recovering from a recent illness, Clara was visiting the mountains for a brief vacation before her wedding to a young soldier. Although Clara was wearing the soldier's engagement ring and a wedding date had been set, it did not discourage 16-year-old Thomas Wolfe from falling in love with her.

Wolfe's infatuation for Clara Paul remained unrequited and

he later claimed he never got over her. "Did you know I fell in love when I was sixteen with a girl who was twenty-one," Wolfe wrote Margaret Roberts in 1924. "Yes, honestly—desperately in love. And I've never quite got over it. The girl married, you know: she died of influenza a year or two later. I've forgotten what she looked like, except that her hair was corn-colored."[4] Two weeks after Clara Paul left the Old Kentucky Home, she married Wallace M. Martin, eventually became the mother of two sons, and then died in 1920.

Clara Elizabeth Paul, ca. 1913, four years before she met Thomas Wolfe. "A nice young boy, here, the son of my landlady, has a crush on me," Miss Paul wrote from Julia Wolfe's boardinghouse in 1917. "Of course, I told him right away that I was engaged. I explained that I could never return his feeling. I was real sorry for him. But he seemed to understand. He'll get over it, I feel sure." (*Thomas Wolfe Undergraduate*, 34.)

Photo courtesy of The Thomas Wolfe Collection, Pack Memorial Public Library, Asheville, North Carolina.

Wolfe reluctantly returned to Chapel Hill for the fall term, but then, unexpectedly, began three of the happiest years of his life. Although his freshman year was not an entirely happy one, his sophomore year revealed a remarkably divergent Thomas Wolfe. He had escaped the tumult of his family in Asheville, and his growing recognition as a Big Man on Campus was a source of unbridled joy.

"I suppose I'm a greater surprise to myself than to anyone under the sun," he wrote his mother on October 31, 1917. "I am changing so rapidly that I find myself an evergrowing source of

Henry Horace Williams ("Vergil Weldon" in *Look Homeward, Angel*). Thomas Wolfe wrote Margaret Roberts in 1921 that she was one of "only three great teachers in my short but eventful life." The other two teachers (both at Chapel Hill) were Horace Williams, head of the Department of Philosophy, and Edwin Greenlaw, head of the Department of English. Williams was well known for his contentious nature and eccentricity. Wolfe enrolled in Williams's Philosophy 15, "A Study of Forces That Shape Life," and soon found himself embroiled in wrestling with a diverse variety of philosophical truths.

Photo courtesy of The North Carolina Collection, University of North Carolina Library at Chapel Hill.

interest. Sounds egotistical, doesn't it? College life does more things for one than I would have ever dreamed."[5] In 1935 he recalled: "About this time, I began to write. I was editor of the college paper. . . . I wrote some stories and some poems for the magazine of which I was also a member of the editorial staff. The War was going on then; I was too young to be in service, and I suppose my first attempts creatively may be traced to the direct and patriotic inspiration of the War."[6]

"A Field in Flanders," a patriotic poem, was Thomas Wolfe's first published effort, appearing in the November 1917 issue of the *University of North Carolina Magazine*. The byline read "Thomas Wolfe," but he also used "Thomas Clayton" and "T.C. Wolfe" for other college publications. The March 1918 issue of the *Magazine* contained his fervent poem, "The Challenge," and his first published work of fiction, "A Cullenden of Virginia," a tale of heroism in World War I.

On March 25, 1918, Wolfe was initiated into Pi Kappa Phi, a new social fraternity that sought members on the basis of leadership and scholarship. He began attending a round of fraternity dances and in April joined Sigma Upsilon, a literary fraternity. On May 3 he joined Omega Delta, a fraternity that promoted the intellectual and aesthetic side of college life and focused on the production of plays. By then he had been appointed one of three associate editors of the college annual, *Yackety Yack,* and on May 17 was named associate editor of the *Tar Heel,* the weekly student newspaper. He would become managing editor in his junior year and editor in chief in his senior year, 1919–1920. He enjoyed playing the role of "unwashed genius" and grew neglectful of his appearance. His hair was seldom cut, he arrived late to class, often wearing clothing he had outgrown or worn out. "A genius doesn't have to be immaculate,"[7] he contended.

Rather than return home after his sophomore year in 1918, Wolfe sought a civilian war-job at Langley Field, Newport News, Virginia, as a time checker. He found himself still thinking of Clara Paul, then living in nearby Portsmouth with her husband, but never mustered the courage to call on her. He worked at

The second of Thomas Wolfe's great male teachers was Edwin Greenlaw ("Randolph Ware" in *The Web and the Rock*). During Wolfe's final three years at Chapel Hill, he always enrolled in one of Greenlaw's classes. In his junior year Wolfe enrolled in Greenlaw's English 21, a course in composition based on daily events and current affairs. Greenlaw's students experimented with writing about the world around them, a training that Wolfe would utilize as a novelist.

Photo courtesy of The North Carolina Collection, University of North Carolina Library at Chapel Hill.

Langley Field until July 4, when, consumed by bedbugs and mosquitoes, he resigned his job, although penniless. Fortunately, his brother Fred, stationed at Norfolk, rescued him from near-starvation. That summer he also tried his hand as a carpenter but was fired on his first day because of incompetence.

In September Wolfe went to Asheville for a brief visit before returning to Chapel Hill for the fall term. W.O., ill with inflammatory rheumatism and prostate cancer, had moved from the Woodfin Street house into a large back bedroom of the Old Kentucky Home. Tom's brother Ben, who had been working as the circulation manager for Winston-Salem's *Twin City Sentinel*, had also returned to Julia's boardinghouse. Tom found his brother in a bitter, despondent mood. Ben had been rejected for military service, possibly because of inactive pulmonary tuberculosis. He blamed his mother for his condition because she accepted tuberculars at the Old Kentucky Home, defending them blindly—as long as they paid their room and board.

Wolfe had returned to Chapel Hill for only a few weeks when he received the news of Ben's desperate illness. Their sister Effie

Ben Wolfe's death, elegized in *Look Homeward, Angel,* provided the most evocative passage in the novel:

"We can believe in the nothingness of life, we can believe in the nothingness of death and of life after death—but who can believe in the nothingness of Ben? Like Apollo, who did his penance to the high god in the sad house of King Admetus, he came, a god with broken feet, into the gray hovel of this world. And he lived here a stranger, trying to recapture the music of the lost world, trying to recall the great forgotten language, the lost faces, the stone, the leaf, the door."

—*Look Homeward, Angel,* 557

Photo courtesy of The North Carolina Collection, University of North Carolina Library at Chapel Hill, and the Estate of Thomas Wolfe.

and her children had visited the Old Kentucky Home and had spread Spanish influenza. Julia sent Tom a telegram asking him to return at once, that Ben had pneumonia. Tom took the train to Asheville, arriving at the Old Kentucky Home in the early morning. Resentful of Julia's parsimony and blaming her for neglecting him during his illness, Ben refused to allow her inside the sickroom. "Get out! Out! Don't want you,"[8] Ben tells his mother in *Look Homeward, Angel*. Only shortly before he died, after he lost consciousness, did Julia take her place at the bed beside him. According to his death certificate, Ben died at four o'clock in the morning, October 19, 1918, of "Pneumonia following Influenza." Thomas Wolfe later stated that "the Asheville I knew died for me when Ben died. I have never forgotten him and I never shall. I think that his death affected me more than any other event in my life."[9]

Thomas Wolfe in *The Return of Buck Gavin*, 1919. The little play contained traces of Wolfe's innate poetic genius: the mountain outlaw has returned to certain death to place violets over his fallen comrade's grave.

Photo courtesy of The Thomas Wolfe Collection, Pack Memorial Public Library, Asheville, North Carolina.

After Ben's funeral Wolfe returned to Chapel Hill. Earlier that September he had joined the newly organized Carolina Playmakers, Frederick H. Koch's course in playwriting. Koch emphasized the importance of writing "folk plays," and Wolfe was an eager participant. The prime purpose of the Playmakers was to produce and promote original plays depicting North Carolina life and people. Wolfe returned to his mountain roots—his first play, *The Return of Buck Gavin*, was hastily written in three hours at one sitting, and was one of the first plays to be presented by the Playmakers. It was produced on March 14 and 15, 1919, and because no actor could be found to convincingly portray Buck Gavin, the tall mountain outlaw, Wolfe himself was enlisted to play the title role.

Wolfe continued writing one-act plays for the duration of his time at Chapel Hill. His second play, *Deferred Payment*, was published in the June 1919 issue of the *Magazine*. Two more plays would be published: *The Streets of Durham, or Dirty Work at the Cross Roads* (University of North Carolina *Tar Baby*, 18 November 1919), and *Concerning Honest Bob* (the *Magazine*, May 1920). In later years Wolfe grew ashamed of these early efforts, explaining, "I had not learned to work, and what I wrote did not represent the best in me."[10] Another effort, the folk play *The Third Night*, was produced by the Playmakers on December 12 and 13, 1919 (with Wolfe once again in the cast).

Wolfe's crowning glory as a student at Chapel Hill occurred in the spring of 1919, when, along with six others, he was elected to the honor society the Golden Fleece, the highest honor that could be bestowed at the University of North Carolina. At the

Frederick H. Koch, founder of the Carolina Playmakers. "I shall never forget his first performance," Koch later wrote of Wolfe's portrayal of Buck Gavin. "With free mountain stride, his dark eyes blazing, he became the hunted outlaw of the Great Smokies. There was something uncanny in his acting of the part—something of the pent-up fury of his highland forbears." (*Carolina Folk-Plays*, Second Series, 40.)

Photo courtesy of The North Carolina Collection, University of North Carolina Library at Chapel Hill.

Thomas Wolfe with other members of Pi Kappa Phi at the University of North Carolina, 1919–1920. Wolfe standing, top row, center.

Photo courtesy of The Thomas Wolfe Collection, Pack Memorial Public Library, Asheville, North Carolina.

end of this, his junior year, he won the university's esteemed Worth Prize in Philosophy for his essay, "The Crisis in Industry," a study examining the labor problems that followed the signing of the Armistice. The essay was printed as a pamphlet by the university.

When Wolfe returned for his senior year, he found himself busier than ever. As editor in chief of the *Tar Heel*, he slept little more than five hours a night in order to juggle all of his activities. "I hate to leave this place," he wrote on May 17, 1920, a month before graduation, to Lora French, a girl he had romanced in Asheville. "It's mighty hard. It's the oldest of the state universities and there's an atmosphere here that's fine and good. Other universities have larger student bodies and bigger and finer buildings, but in Spring there are none, I know, so wonderful by half."[11] Both W.O. and Julia went to their son's graduation and attended several closing exercises, although W.O. was too weak to attend the commencement ceremony on June 16.

That summer Wolfe declined a teaching job at the Bingham Military School, a private preparatory school in Asheville, worrying that he would risk sacrificing a writing career to become a "small-town pedant."[12] Once again his family began arguing about his future. W.O. was still insistent upon his son becoming a lawyer, although by now he was growing too enfeebled to care. "Don't bother me with it,"[13] he told Tom.

But now Tom had set his sights on graduate study at Harvard. He had been urged to attend Harvard by Frederick Koch who had himself studied playwriting under George Pierce Baker in his renowned 47 Workshop. Wolfe was convinced that his dream of becoming a dramatist would be realized at Harvard and he besieged his mother to pay for his first semester, even suggesting the money be deducted from his father's will. Julia relented and agreed to pay his way for the first year. She in fact ended up paying for all three of his years at Harvard. However, as Tom soon found out, his mother was rarely eager to part with money, and her checks were often delayed or arrived at the last minute.

Wolfe applied in August 1920 for admission to Harvard's Graduate School of Arts and Sciences and was accepted in a letter dated September 13. He traveled first to Baltimore, where his father was receiving radium treatments at Johns Hopkins Hospital. Wolfe noted that his father's life seemed to be "hanging on by one rusty hinge, but hanging—As all the doctors: 'He will not live through the night' but generally he lives through the week— the doctors say it's extraordinary."[14] After saying good-bye, Tom boarded the train for New York City, where he visited for several days, and then went on to his final destinations of Boston and Cambridge. He later mythologized his transition from the South to the North in his second novel, *Of Time and the River*:

> Down in the city's central web, the boy could distinguish faintly the line of the rails, and see the engine smoke above the railroad yards, and as he looked, he heard far off that haunting sound and prophecy of youth and of his life—the bell, the wheel, the wailing whistle—and the train.
>
> Then he turned swiftly and went to meet it—and all the new lands, morning, and the shining city. . . .[15]

NOTES

1. *Letters*, 4.

2. *Look Homeward, Angel*, 391.

3. *Ibid.*, 394–395.

4. *Letters*, 66.

5. *The Letters of Thomas Wolfe to His Mother*, 4.

6. Thomas Wolfe, *The Autobiography of an American Novelist*, Leslie Field, ed. (Cambridge, MA: Harvard University Press, 1983), 104.

7. *Thomas Wolfe Undergraduate*, 41.

8. *Look Homeward, Angel*, 547.

9. *Letters*, 178.

10. Elizabeth Nowell. *Thomas Wolfe: A Biography*, (Garden City, NY: Doubleday & Company, Inc., 1960), 47.

11. *Letters*, 8.

12. *The Letters of Thomas Wolfe to His Mother*, 7.

13. *The Autobiographical Outline*, 58.

14. *Ibid.*, 44.

15. Thomas Wolfe. *Of Time and the River* (New York: Charles Scribner's Sons, 1935), 86.

3

Harvard, New York University, Europe, *Look Homeward, Angel* 1920 – 1929

Do you know, all that really matters right now is the knowledge that I am twenty-three, and a golden May is here. The feeling of immortality in youth is upon me. I am young, and I can never die. Don't tell me that I can. Wait until I'm thirty. Then I'll believe you.
— *The Letters of Thomas Wolfe*, 68

Thomas Wolfe at Harvard, ca. 1920–1921.

Photo courtesy of The North Carolina Collection, University of North Carolina Library at Chapel Hill, and the Estate of Thomas Wolfe.

THOMAS WOLFE entered the Graduate School of Arts and Sciences at Harvard University in September 1920. For three years he enrolled in the same playwriting course, English 47, with George Pierce Baker ("Professor James Graves Hatcher" in *Of Time and the River*). Baker had instructed a score of playwrights and directors who then embarked upon successful careers on Broadway. (Eugene O'Neill was a 47 Workshop alumnus.) Wolfe's Harvard years were frequently lonely, although he often saw his uncle Henry A. Westall and his aunt Laura in nearby Medford, spending many Sundays and holidays with them. He became close friends with Baker's assistant, Kenneth Raisbeck, who shared with Wolfe his knowledge of art and Boston nightlife. Wolfe indulged in several romances in Boston and Cambridge ("The brooding romance in my heart— In love with every waitress"[1]), but he no longer possessed the gregariousness of his student days at Chapel Hill.

Wolfe flung himself fervently into his work as a playwright. Baker's 47 Workshop became "the rock to which his life was anchored, the rudder of his destiny, the sole and all-sufficient reason for his being here."[2] His first play finished at Harvard was a folk play about North Carolina, *The Mountains*. He had started the play at Chapel Hill, and once again, perhaps still under Frederick Koch's influence, began writing about his mountain environment. Baker was proud of Wolfe's submission and told the class that Wolfe had accomplished in one act what three-act plays had failed to do. A trial performance of *The Mountains* was presented at the 47 Workshop's rehearsal room before members of the class on January 25, 1921. Baker was so impressed that he encouraged Wolfe to write a three-act version.

By the end of his first year, Wolfe completed—with high grades—three of four courses required for a Master of Arts degree: English 33 (American Literature), English 47, and elementary French. He needed an additional course to complete his M.A., but in no hurry, he planned to return to the 47 Workshop in the fall. During summer vacation he considered working his

Professor George Pierce Baker in 1920. Thomas Wolfe wrote his mother that Baker "is the greatest authority on the drama in America and in the last six years he has developed in this class some of the best dramatists in the country, several of whom have plays on Broadway now. I was in the depths of despair at the time but his talk has lifted me up again." (*The Letters of Thomas Wolfe to His Mother,* 13.)

Photo courtesy of The Thomas Wolfe Collection, Pack Memorial Public Library, Asheville, North Carolina.

way across the Atlantic aboard a transatlantic steamer as a stoker, but finally decided to enroll in summer school. Just before the fall term began, he learned that his mother had again taken his father to Johns Hopkins Hospital for radium treatments. He joined them at Baltimore and persuaded Julia to finance one more year of graduate work.

On October 21 and 22, 1921, the 47 Workshop staged *The Mountains* at the Agassiz Theatre at Radcliffe College. The production was not a success, and Wolfe was both disappointed and angered by the criticisms. The most frequent criticism was that the audience found it depressing, to which Wolfe responded to Baker, "If the audience is depressed over my play, I am depressed over my audience."[3]

In early February 1922 Wolfe received a note from the secretary of the graduate school informing him that he would receive his M.A. with distinction once he completed the French requirement. Although his first attempt to pass the French exam was unsuccessful, he succeeded in May. When the term was over, he had completed the four courses required for the degree, and received credit for two more. His second year in the 47 Workshop did not count for the degree, because not more than one composition course counted, but by now Wolfe's hopes, dreams, and ambitions were fastened on becoming a successful playwright.

Although Wolfe received his M.A. degree in June 1922, he planned to return in the fall to work with Professor Baker for one more year. A few days before commencement, Wolfe was suddenly summoned to Asheville where his father was dying. Wolfe left Cambridge on June 19. When the train stopped at Morganton, 50 miles east of Asheville, he bought the early edition of the Asheville newspaper and learned of his father's death. W.O. had died of cancer shortly after midnight on June 20, in the Old Kentucky Home. Getting off at the Biltmore depot, Wolfe ran weeping along the platform, informing his waiting sister Mabel, "You don't have to tell me. I read it in the paper." [4]

Matters were unsettled after W.O.'s death, but Wolfe managed to secure his mother's support to enroll in the 47 Workshop for a third year. During the summer in Asheville, he began writing *Niggertown*, which later became *Welcome to Our City*. The new play would focus on "Greed, greed, greed," he wrote Margaret Roberts, "deliberate, crafty, motivated—masking under the guise of civic associations for municipal betterment. The disgusting spectacle of thousands of industrious and accomplished liars, engaged in the mutual and systematic pursuit of their profession. . . ." [5] The town of "accomplished liars" Wolfe called "Altamont."

Wolfe returned to Harvard in September and rented a room at 21 Trowbridge Street. According to a member of the 47 Workshop, Wolfe submitted the first acts of six different plays to Baker. By December 1922 he had finished the prologue and first act of *Niggertown* and was at work on the second act, hoping to finish the entire three acts by Christmas.

On May 11 and 12, 1923, the 47 Workshop staged *Welcome to Our City* at the Agassiz Theatre. The curtain went up at 8 P.M. and did not go down until midnight. The 10-scene play was "the most ambitious thing—in size, at any rate—the Workshop has ever attempted," Wolfe wrote his mother, "there are ten scenes, over thirty people, and seven changes of setting."[6] That spring, in a letter to Professor Baker, Wolfe stated his lofty theatrical ambitions: "I have written this play with thirty-odd *named* characters because it required it, not because I didn't know how to save paint. Some day I'm going to write a play with fifty, eighty, a hundred people—a whole town, a whole race, a whole epoch—for my soul's ease and comfort."[7]

Welcome to Our City was not a success and did not win the award for best play written in the Workshop that Wolfe had hoped for. However, Professor Baker was well aware of Wolfe's talents and continued to encourage him to persist in writing plays. (Baker was disappointed when Wolfe started teaching in 1924.) Wolfe was encouraged by Baker's opinion that he should cut *Welcome to Our City* and submit it to the Theatre Guild. "I know this now," he wrote his mother, "I am inevitable, I sincerely believe. The only thing that can stop me now is insanity, disease or death."[8]

In August Wolfe revised *Welcome to Our City* and submitted it to the Theatre Guild. He returned to Asheville to await the Guild's decision (which did not come for four months—he later claimed he was "on the verge of madness and collapse"[9] while waiting). After a long visit with his family, in November he took a job in New York City, soliciting donations from North Carolina alumni for the Graham Memorial Building at the University of North Carolina. He did not enroll in the 47 Workshop that fall. By late 1923 he had served his apprenticeship under Baker and while waiting for a professional production on Broadway, he realized he would have to support himself. In December the Theatre Guild declined *Welcome to Our City*, although they informed Wolfe that they would reconsider if he tightened and shortened it. But Wolfe made little attempt to revise and resubmit the play.

Through the Harvard appointment office, Wolfe learned of a new opening at a branch of New York University, Washington Square College. On January 10, 1924, he wrote Homer A. Watt, chairman of the English Department, admitting that he had no teaching experience and intended to devote his life to playwriting. Watt was impressed with Wolfe's earnest manner and felt his work with Professor Baker constituted enough credentials. Wolfe began teaching at Washington Square College on February 6, 1924, and continued intermittently until January 17, 1930.

Wolfe was assigned three courses in English composition. He was promised 90 students (although 104 were accepted), eight to ten hours of classroom work, and 26 hours a week of theme reading. His first year's salary was $1,800 and this was raised the following year to $2,000. As his students could attest, Thomas Wolfe was a severe marker. During his first year, he gave only three A's to 104 students, six B's, 53 C's, 21 D's, nine F's, and two "absent" marks when only grades of C or better counted as grades for graduation. Wolfe accomplished little creative work while teaching, finding it impossible to teach and write at the same time. For the most part his time was consumed by correcting papers.

In March Wolfe decided to travel to Europe after the summer term was over. Professor Baker had convinced him that traveling in Europe and absorbing its culture was necessary for his training as a writer. Wolfe's initial plan was to take a leave of absence from teaching and write undisturbed while traveling through Europe for two months. He resolved to write 1,500 words a day while abroad. He maintained his resolve but did not return to teach until the fall of the following year.

On October 25 Wolfe sailed aboard the *Lancastria* for his first of seven trips to Europe. He caught his first glimpse of English soil on November 4, the little harbor town of Plymouth, but his destination of London was still 200 miles away. He made good use of the ocean journey by recording his thoughts, observations, and memories. This manuscript would grow over the next five months as he extended his stay in Europe. He titled it "Passage to England." It soon became a profane blend of fact and fiction containing numerous unsavory details about Asheville. "Passage to England" was not published during Wolfe's lifetime, but a small, innocuous excerpt, "London Tower," appeared in the *Asheville Citizen* on July 19, 1925.

Wolfe spent November in England, then continued to Paris. On his third day in Paris, his old valise containing the uncompleted manuscript of *Mannerhouse* was stolen. He had been working on the play for more than a year. The manuscript, he wrote his mother, "had become a part of me. I don't think you can understand my feeling quite, but nothing has hit me as hard as this since papa's death."[10] The manuscript was the only one in existence, and Wolfe had no alternative but to rewrite it. Finished the first week of January 1925, the new *Mannerhouse* he claimed was "'bigger and better' than the old one—I believe the best thing I've ever done."[11]

By the time this photo was dated and stamped, December 22, 1924, Thomas Wolfe possessed a deep baritone voice and had reached a height of 6'6". His extreme height intensified his painful self-consciousness: "The world this man would live in is the world of six feet six," he later wrote, "and that is the strangest and most lonely world there is." (*Complete Short Stories*, 241.)

Photo courtesy of The North Carolina Collection, University of North Carolina Library at Chapel Hill, and the Estate of Thomas Wolfe.

As early as November 1924, Homer A. Watt was attempting to lure Wolfe back for the semester beginning in February 1925 and ending after summer school in September. Watt offered a salary increase of $200, but Wolfe was enjoying his adventures in Italy, England, and France too much and was in no hurry to return to teaching. However, by June 1925 when he was nearly out of money and knew his mother would not continue to support his travels, he negotiated with Professor Watt. Watt asked Wolfe to report by September 21 and informed him recitations were to begin the next day. Wolfe was assigned nine hours of freshman English and an introduction to literature for teachers.

Wolfe left Europe in late August aboard the *Olympic*. On August 25, the day before he was to arrive in New York, he met Aline Bernstein, a renowned New York City stage and costume designer. Nineteen years older than Wolfe, and married, Mrs. Bernstein became his mistress for the next five years and the great love of his life. She supplied Wolfe with not only the emotional support and belief in his talent that allowed him to write *Look Homeward, Angel,* but financial assistance as well. She was married to a wealthy stockbroker, Theodore Bernstein, and had raised two children, but was no longer maintaining an exclusive sexual relationship with her husband.

Aline Bernstein, ca. 1930s. "My tender and golden love, you were my other loneliness, the only clasp of hand and heart that I had," Thomas Wolfe wrote Mrs. Bernstein in 1928. "I was a stranger, alone and lost in the wilderness, and I found you." (*My Other Loneliness,* 194.)

Photo courtesy of the Aldo P. Magi Collection.

Wolfe resumed teaching in September and by October had developed a close relationship with Mrs. Bernstein. For a year and a half, it would be near perfect for them. During the winter of 1925–1926, Wolfe moved into a loft at 13 East Eighth Street that Mrs. Bernstein also rented as a studio while still maintaining her Park Avenue residence with her husband and children. During their many talks, Wolfe and Mrs. Bernstein shared their childhood reminiscences. Urged on by his mistress, Wolfe wisely decided to abandon playwriting and instead write an autobiographical novel.

On June 23 Wolfe boarded the *Berengaria* for Europe. Mrs. Bernstein had offered to finance the trip once his teaching duties were finished. She also promised he could give up teaching and she would support him until he was ready to return to New York. By the time he sailed, Mrs. Bernstein had already departed for Europe on business; they were reunited in Paris. They traveled through France and England, and in Paris, Wolfe began writing notes and phrases for the novel about his life that he first called "The Building of a Wall." He began jotting down ideas in a plain tablet and later a hardcover composition book. After completing these notes, he began writing in large accounting ledgers supplied by Mrs. Bernstein, who believed this was the only way Wolfe could keep track of what he had written. He eventually filled 17 ledgers. He wrote in longhand, favoring Eberhard Faber Blackwing pencils. He believed his hands were too big and unwieldy to operate a typewriter and hired typists or secretaries to type his manuscripts.

On December 22 Wolfe ended his trip and sailed home aboard the *Majestic*. He settled back into the Eighth Street studio he shared with Mrs. Bernstein and for six months continued working on his novel. After a third trip to Europe in July 1927, he resumed teaching at New York University. He moved out of the Eighth Street loft and into a more spacious apartment at 263 W. Eleventh Street, once again sharing space with Mrs. Bernstein. Here, on March 31, 1928, he completed the manuscript now called "O Lost." After several attempts to market it herself, Mrs. Bernstein submitted the mammoth manuscript (via her chauffeur) to literary agent Madeleine Boyd. Mrs. Boyd was wildly enthusiastic, and after reading only one-third of the novel, jumped to her feet, shouting, "A genius, I have discovered a genius!"[12] Nonetheless, she warned Wolfe that cuts were needed. On May 20 Wolfe engaged Mrs. Boyd as his literary agent. Despite Mrs. Boyd's discovery of a genius, it would take seven months to find a publisher. Meanwhile, Wolfe began working on a new novel, "The River People," which he planned to be a more conventional, commercial book, a love story about a wealthy young painter and an Austrian girl. This contrived plot did not hold his interest, although he continued working sporadically on it for most of 1928.

On June 30 Wolfe sailed aboard the *Rotterdam*, landing at Boulogne, and then visited France, Belgium, and Germany. On September 30 he was injured in Munich during a drunken brawl with German revelers at the Oktoberfest. He was hospitalized until October 4, spending his 28th birthday as a patient. His nose was broken and he suffered several deep head wounds as well as a few small facial wounds. But then his fortunes changed. In what was certainly the most momentous event of his life, he received a letter in Vienna from Maxwell E. Perkins, legendary editor at Charles Scribner's Sons, asking him to return to New York to discuss "O Lost."

Maxwell Perkins never forgot his first meeting with Thomas Wolfe on January 2, 1929: "Wolfe arrived in New York and stood in the doorway of my boxstall of an office leaning against the door jamb. When I looked up and saw his wild hair and bright countenance—although he was so altogether different physically—I thought of Shelley. *He* was fair, but his hair was wild, and his face was bright and his head disproportionately small."[13] Perkins did not commit Scribner's until all details could be agreed upon, and made a number of suggestions for Wolfe to consider over the following days. The wait was not long:

Maxwell Evarts Perkins (1884–1947). "Mrs. Ernest Boyd left with us, some weeks ago, the manuscript of your novel, 'O Lost,'" Perkins wrote Thomas Wolfe on October 22, 1928. "I do not know whether it would be possible to work out a plan by which it might be worked into a form publishable by us, but I do know that, setting the practical aspects of the matter aside, it is a very remarkable thing, and that no editor could read it without being excited by it and filled with admiration by many passages in it and sections of it." (*Editor to Author*, 61.)

Photo courtesy of the North Carolina Department of Cultural Resources.

on January 7 Wolfe and Perkins met, and Perkins agreed to publish "O Lost." The contract was signed on January 9. Wolfe kept the contract in his inner breast coat pocket with the advance for $450 pinned to it (a 10 percent commission had already been paid to Madeleine Boyd). He walked around the city, taking the papers out, gazing at them tenderly, sometimes kissing them. He walked 80 blocks before realizing how far he had gone.

Wolfe, who had resumed teaching while revising the manuscript, proposed to revise and correct 100 pages at a time and deliver 100 pages every week. Over the next four months, he worked closely with Perkins. The original manuscript totaled 1,114 pages and contained 330,000 words. Although during the initial revision it was reduced by 95,000 words, Wolfe added 5,000 more with new transitions. The net reduction was roughly 90,000 words with a total of 147 cuts.

In April the editorial staff asked Wolfe to select a better title. Wolfe jotted down dozens, including "The Buried Life," "The

Thomas Wolfe, summer 1929; publicity photo by Doris Ulmann for *Look Homeward, Angel.* As he corrected proofs for *Look Homeward, Angel,* Wolfe wrote a preface at Scribner's suggestion to protect himself from lawsuits. In the note "To the Reader" he insisted that his book was "a fiction, and that he meditated no man's portrait here." In truth, the resemblance between living persons and fictional characters was rarely accidental.

Photo courtesy of the North Carolina Department of Cultural Resources.

Childhood of Dr. Faust," "Remembering Home," and "The Search for the Lost Boy." Finally, after several lists, we find "Look Homeward, Angel." In his notebook he wrote, "Put into final scene of book: 'Look Homeward, Angel, now, and melt with ruth.'"[14] Although Wolfe intended to work the quotation from Milton's "Lycidas" into the novel, he never succeeded in employing the quotation in the final manuscript.

On September 7 Wolfe made a short visit to Asheville, his last until 1937. He found the city full of interest in his forthcoming book but could not avoid the usual tensions in his family. "We get one another crazy—I've been here a week and I'm about ready for a padded cell," he wrote Maxwell Perkins on September 14. Although Wolfe told Perkins "My family knows what it's all about,"[15] in truth, he discussed little about *Look Homeward, Angel* with anyone. Whether, as he later claimed, Asheville's hostile reaction to the novel was a complete surprise is open to dispute. After he left his family behind, on the train going north, he forlornly jotted down in his notebook: "Shall I ever come back to my home, ever again?"[16]

Wolfe returned to New York and resumed teaching. *Look Homeward, Angel* was published on October 18 and caused an uproar in Asheville. The novel was condemned from street corner to pulpit and banned from the public library. Wolfe received anonymous letters "full of vilification and abuse, one which threatened to kill me if I came back home, others which were merely obscene. One venerable old lady, whom I had known all my life, wrote me—in an extraordinary letter which ran to eight pages, which never stopped once to draw a breath—that she wondered how I could have such a crime upon my soul, and added that although she had never believed in lynch law, she would do nothing to prevent a mob from dragging that 'big overgrown karkus' across the public square."[17]

There are more than 200 characters in *Look Homeward, Angel*, all easily identifiable citizens of Asheville. "The only reason we weren't tarred and feathered was because Tom didn't spare us in the book,"[18] Wolfe's sister Mabel later stated. Margaret Roberts was so angered by the derogatory portrait of her husband that she fired off an angry letter to Wolfe, declaring, "You have crucified your family and devastated mine."[19] She did not write to him again for seven years. "It is long, exciting, and has a number of very stark passages," Mrs. Roberts reported shortly after *Look Homeward, Angel* was published. "The book is about Asheville people, some of it true, and some fiction, but all convincingly written, and so localized that any inhabitant of Asheville can identify every spot and person."[20]

Surprisingly, the novel elicited praise from both the *Asheville Citizen* and *Asheville Times* (and received rave reviews from nearly everywhere else). Wolfe's family reacted with a mixture of bewilderment, pain, and humiliation. When Julia Wolfe received the novel, she sat down to read it at once, sometimes laughing, sometimes crying. "I suppose I stopped to eat my dinner, but read til three o'clock in the morning," she claimed, "almost finished the book."[21] While Julia and Mabel were horrified by the novel's contents, they remained loyal to their son and brother, neither making public their criticisms. Fred Wolfe was amused by his portrayal as the stutterer, "Luke." But Frank Wolfe admitted he was ready to commit murder if Tom returned to Asheville. (Frank was portrayed as the dissolute "Steve Gant.")

The year 1929 had been momentous for Thomas Wolfe, although some of the success of the novel was tainted by Asheville's adverse reaction. By the end of the year, there was much for which he could be thankful, especially his relationship with Maxwell Perkins. "Young men sometimes believe in the existence of heroic figures, stronger and wiser than themselves, to whom they can turn for an answer to all their vexation and grief," Wolfe wrote Perkins on Christmas Eve. "Later, they must discover that such answers have to come out of their own hearts; but the powerful desire to believe in such figures persists. You are for me such a figure: you are one of the rocks to which my life is anchored."[22]

NOTES

1. *The Autobiographical Outline,* 63.

2. *Of Time and the River,* 130.

3. *Letters,* 20.

4. Nowell, 65.

5. *Letters,* 33.

6. *The Letters of Thomas Wolfe to His Mother,* 38.

7. *Letters,* 41.

8. *The Letters of Thomas Wolfe to His Mother,* 42.

9. *Letters*, 58.

10. *The Letters of Thomas Wolfe to His Mother*, 83.

11. *Ibid.*, 85.

12. Madeleine Boyd. *Thomas Wolfe: The Discovery of a Genius*, Aldo P. Magi, ed. (Thomas Wolfe Society, 1981), 3. Note: Despite Madeleine Boyd's "discovery of a genius," Margaret Roberts must be rightfully credited for first proclaiming Thomas Wolfe a genius (see pp. 16–17 of this volume).

13. Maxwell Perkins, "Thomas Wolfe," *Harvard Library Bulletin* 1:3 (Autumn 1947): 271.

14. *The Notebooks of Thomas Wolfe*, Richard S. Kennedy and Paschal Reeves, eds. (Chapel Hill: University of North Carolina Press, 1970), I, 330.

15. *Letters*, 203. Note: Wolfe's sister Mabel has stated: "I never dreamed—and this opinion I voice for my family: Mama, Fred, Effie, Frank—what would be in the book." (Nowell, 143.)

16. *Notebooks*, I, 370.

17. *The Autobiography of an American Novelist*, 17–18.

18. Nowell, 150.

19. George W. McCoy, "Asheville and Thomas Wolfe," *North Carolina Historical Review* 30:2 (April 1953): 207.

20. Ted Mitchell, "Margaret Roberts Writes to Her Daughter's Roommate," *Thomas Wolfe Review* 18:2 (Fall 1994): 70.

21. *Thomas Wolfe's Letters to His Mother*, John Skally Terry, ed. (New York: Charles Scribner's Sons, 1943), xxviii.

22. *Letters*, 213.

4

Brooklyn and *Of Time and the River*
1930 – 1935

To be a stranger; always to be a stranger.
—*The Notebooks of Thomas Wolfe*, II, 537

Thomas Wolfe, February 19, 1935; passport photo.

Photo courtesy of The North Carolina Collection, University of North Carolina Library at Chapel Hill, and the Estate of Thomas Wolfe.

OOK *HOMEWARD, ANGEL* proved both a critical and commercial success, and Maxwell Perkins was eager for Thomas Wolfe to produce a new novel as soon as possible. After consulting with Charles Scribner III, Perkins offered to subsidize Wolfe by paying him a $4,500 advance on his next novel—the advance to be paid in monthly installments of $250, beginning February 1. Although Wolfe would not draw his first royalties from *Look Homeward, Angel* until spring 1930, on the strength of the advance Perkins arranged, he resigned his teaching post, effective February 6, 1930, and never worked as a teacher again.

During the spring evenings of 1929, as Perkins and Wolfe worked on editing "O Lost," Perkins's influence upon Wolfe grew so great that he replaced Aline Bernstein as Wolfe's mentor. At the end of 1929, Perkins suggested that Wolfe, without informing Mrs. Bernstein, apply for a Guggenheim fellowship, which would enable him to go to Europe and write in isolation with financial security. Wolfe had grown more alienated from Mrs. Bernstein as his fame grew and, in turn, Mrs. Bernstein grew more possessive of him. In March 1930, when he informed her that he had been awarded the Guggenheim and would leave alone for Europe, Mrs. Bernstein felt betrayed for she had been willing to support him while he worked on his new novel. As he prepared to go to Europe, he was determined to exercise his independence and end his relationship with her. Once he reached Europe, he broke off all correspondence, much to Mrs. Bernstein's dismay and pain.

Wolfe sailed aboard the *Volendam* on May 9. Arriving in Paris on May 19, he spent several weeks moving from one hotel to another before finally settling down to work on the manuscript he called "The October Fair." He met and befriended another of Maxwell Perkins's authors, F. Scott Fitzgerald. Wolfe liked Fitzgerald at once, considered him a talented writer, but was distressed at how Fitzgerald was dissipating his career with alcohol. However, Wolfe was pleased when Fitzgerald telegraphed that he had finished reading *Look Homeward, Angel* in 20 consecutive hours. Wolfe hoped that Fitzgerald would repent and lead a better life thereafter.[1] Wolfe himself was a heavy drinker, an abuser of alcohol for all of his adult life, but exercised restraint when writing. "It would be very easy for me to start swilling liquor at present but I am *not* going to do it," he wrote Perkins on July 17, 1930. "I am here to get work done, and in the next three months, I am going to see whether I am a bum or a man."[2]

That summer Wolfe traveled in Switzerland before settling in London in October. He was having "second book trouble" and recorded in his pocket journal, "I am all broken up in fragments myself at present and all that I can write is fragments. The man is his work: if the work is whole, the man must be whole."[3] Along with his chronic depression, he was feeling guilty for deserting Aline Bernstein so ruthlessly, especially since he was using her early life and memories of New York for another projected novel, "The Good Child's River." (Wolfe frequently worked on several projected novels at one time.)

At the end of February 1931 Wolfe sailed home on the *Europa*. In March he discovered that Mrs. Bernstein had suffered an emotional and physical breakdown and was hospitalized. She partially blamed Wolfe for his callous treatment of her. "Apparently to love you as I do is an insanity—I am having a great fight in my self," she wrote from New York Doctors Hospital in March. "The way I love you will never stop, but I know now that you will no longer have me nor hold me dear. It is impossible for me to cope with every day life for a little while. You know not what you do."[4]

In March Wolfe rented the first of four apartments in Brooklyn, once again repeating his habit of moving from one apartment to another, rather than settling in a permanent home. He moved into 40 Verandah Place and settled down to work steadily on a variety of material (usually standing while he wrote, using the top of a refrigerator for his desk). He continued working on

"The October Fair" and "The Good Child's River," and over the following year worked on new projects as well: "A Portrait of Bascom Hawke," "The Web of Earth," "No Door," and the aborted novel "K-19."

In November 1931 Wolfe rented a third-floor apartment at 111 Columbia Heights in Brooklyn, where he lived until August 1932. His definitive break with Aline Bernstein occurred here in mid-January 1932 when Julia Wolfe visited. When Mrs. Bernstein called on Wolfe to bring money he had requested for a loan, a bitter fight ensued. Wolfe began arguing with Mrs. Bernstein about a lawsuit involving Madeleine Boyd's embezzlement of his German royalties and illogically blamed Mrs. Bernstein for introducing him to Mrs. Boyd. Entering into the fray, Julia Wolfe denounced Mrs. Bernstein's love for Wolfe and humiliated her by attacking her relationship with her husband. Both Julia and Wolfe bodily removed Mrs. Bernstein from the apartment.

Mrs. Bernstein responded to the "horrid cruel phrases of your mother and yourself" with a blistering letter: "I had five one hundred dollar bills in my purse yesterday, which you asked me to bring you Monday morning," she wrote on January 14. "When I left you today, I took one out and threw it over the Brooklyn Bridge, I thought if they cannot understand how I love you, here is something to appease the Gods your people worship." She claimed she would continue over the next four days to throw a hundred-dollar bill over the bridge into the river, "just to show God I don't come from Asheville."[5] Mrs. Bernstein and Wolfe did not meet again for two years. Julia Wolfe never forgave Mrs. Bernstein for loving her son: "If there had been less of her," she once complained, "there would have been more of him."[6]

But during this period of turmoil, Wolfe's literary career, once lagging with no successor to his first novel, resumed with two important publications. In April 1932 his novella about his uncle Henry Westall, "A Portrait of Bascom Hawke," was published in *Scribner's Magazine*. This first publication since *Look Homeward, Angel* tied for first place in a $5,000 short novel competition sponsored by *Scribner's Magazine*. In May he finished another novella for *Scribner's Magazine*, "The Web of Earth," based on a long and complex story Julia had told him during her Brooklyn visit. After working hard all summer, he took a few days off at the beginning of October and visited his father's relatives in York Springs, Pennsylvania, meeting several people who remembered W.O. In late October, overworked to the extent that he "just gave out completely," he wrote his mother he "had never been so fagged out mentally, physically, and every other way. I got on a boat and went to Bermuda, which was a bad thing to do because the place is terribly expensive, and I did not like it."[7]

In April 1933 Wolfe delivered a large portion of "The October Fair" to Maxwell Perkins, changing its name to "Time and the River" (the "of" was added later), a title, he explained, meaning "Memory and Change."[8] In May he signed a contract with a deadline of delivering the complete manuscript on August 1, 1933. However, once he spent his advances for "Time and the River," he quickly began running out of money.

Thomas Wolfe on vacation in Vermont, 1933. In September Wolfe took a much needed vacation to Vermont with author Robert Raynolds. "We have done considerable tramping around on country roads also, eating at farmhouses, and going wherever we wanted to go, and I feel better than I have felt in months," Wolfe wrote Julia Wolfe from Montpelier on September 13. (*The Letters of Thomas Wolfe to His Mother*, 212.)

Photo by permission of the Houghton Library, Harvard University, and the Estate of Thomas Wolfe.

In November, at Perkins's suggestion, Wolfe gave several pieces from his manuscript to Elizabeth Nowell, a young woman who had left the editorial staff of *Scribner's Magazine* for an apprenticeship in the literary agency of Maxim Lieber. Miss Nowell was to edit and cut the manuscript and sell the stories to magazines other than *Scribner's*. Miss Nowell avoided becoming the mother figure that Margaret Roberts and Aline Bernstein had been and she did not allow a romantic relationship to develop. "Tom was always horny as hell," Miss Nowell later remembered, "and you had to keep him at arm's length."[9] Miss Nowell became an important force in Wolfe's literary development, teaching him about editing and focusing his work. Her frequent sales of Wolfe's work greatly boosted his low morale and financed him through the Great Depression.

The deadline for delivering "Time and the River" lapsed in August 1933, but on December 14 Wolfe delivered the last batch

Elizabeth Nowell with her daughter Clara, in 1943. Thomas Wolfe never regretted engaging Miss Nowell as his literary agent, and she soon became one of his closest friends and confidants. Even Wolfe's death did not end Miss Nowell's commitment to him. In 1956 she produced the painstakingly researched *The Letters of Thomas Wolfe*. Two years later, racing with time and her impending death, she worked on the final chapters of her Wolfe biography from her hospital bed, mailing revisions to her 15-year-old daughter, Clara, to type and mail to Wolfe's last editor, Edward Aswell.

Photo courtesy of Clara Stites.

of rough draft. He was aware that much needed to be added to and subtracted from his manuscript and he wished for more time to arrange and sort out the material. Perkins advised Wolfe to concentrate on the first portion of the manuscript (the protagonist leaving the South for Harvard) and to postpone the love story for a later volume. The protagonist reclaimed the name "Eugene Gant," and the new novel continued Eugene's adventures first begun in *Look Homeward, Angel.*

When *Of Time and the River* was published in 1935, it was to have been the second in a series of six books of which, Wolfe claimed, the first four had already been written and the first two, *Look Homeward, Angel* and *Of Time and the River*, published. The title of the whole work, when completed, was to have been *Of Time and the River.*

After working alone until late afternoon, Wolfe went into Manhattan and met Perkins every evening to cut the manuscript and to fill in gaps as well as expand episodes. In September 1934, without Wolfe's knowledge, Perkins sent the last half of *Of Time and the River* to the printers while Wolfe was at the Chicago World's Fair. When informed by Perkins that proof was already coming in, the horrified Wolfe told his editor, "You can't do it . . . the book is not yet finished, I must have six months more on it."[10] Perkins answered that if he were to allow Wolfe six more months, after that he would demand another six months, and then six months more, and the book would never be finished to the author's satisfaction. Wolfe later complained to Perkins that "the book, like Caesar, was from its mother's womb untimely ripped—like King Richard, brought into the world 'scarce half made up.'"[11]

When *Of Time and the River* was published on March 8, 1935, Wolfe had already left for Europe aboard the *Ile de France.* During the ocean voyage, his spirits "sank lower and lower, reaching, I think, the lowest state of hopeless depression they had ever known."[12] Once he reached Europe, he received a cablegram from Perkins reassuring him: "Magnificent reviews, somewhat critical in ways expected, full of greatest praise."[13] But Perkins's cable did not reassure Wolfe, and upon arriving in Paris, he wandered around the city, drinking heavily. "In Paris I couldn't sleep at all," he later wrote Perkins, "I walked the streets from night to morning and was in the worst shape I have ever been in in my life." He then proceeded to describe a nightmarish hallucination he had experienced:

> I came home to my hotel one night—or rather at daybreak one morning—tried to get off to sleep—and had the horrible experience of seeming to disintegrate into at least six people—I was in bed and suddenly it seemed these other shapes of myself were moving *out* of me—all around me— one of them touched me by the arm—another was talking in my ear—others walking around the room—and suddenly I would come to with a terrific jerk and all of them would rush back into me again. I can swear to you I was not asleep—it was one of the strangest and most horrible experiences I've ever had.[14]

Wolfe could no longer control his paranoia and fears, and on March 13 sent the following telegram: "Dear Max: To-day if I mistake not is Wednesday March thirteenth. I can remember almost nothing of last six days. You are the best friend I have. I can face blunt fact better than damnable incertitude. Give me the straight plain truth."[15] Perkins cabled the next day: "Grand excited reception in reviews. Talked of everywhere as truly great book. All comparisons with greatest writers. Enjoy yourself with light heart."[16] Perkins's answer satisfied Wolfe and a letter from Perkins with excerpts from the reviews followed.

After traveling in England and Holland, Wolfe arrived in Berlin on May 7, where he was lionized as a great new American writer. He lived like a prince, spending the German royalties due to him but prohibited by Nazi monetary restrictions from leaving the country. His German publisher, Ernst Rowohlt, arranged for newspaper interviews, magazine articles, photos, and invitations to lavish parties.

Thomas Wolfe in Berlin, May 1935. "Byron, they say, awoke one morning at the age of twenty-four, and found himself a famous man," Wolfe wrote in his essay *Writing and Living.* "Well, I had to wait some ten years longer, but the day came when I walked at morning through the Brandenburger Gate, and into the enchanted avenues of the faery green Tiergarten, and found that fame—or so it seemed to me—had come to me." (*The Autobiography of an American Novelist,* 140.)

Photo courtesy of the North Carolina Department of Cultural Resources.

Upon leaving Germany, Wolfe traveled to Denmark before sailing home aboard the *Bremen* on June 27. By the time he arrived in New York on July 4, the success of *Of Time and the River* was assured. He was surprised to find a crowd of reporters waiting at the dock to interview him. Maxwell Perkins was also waiting there. Unfortunately, Perkins had news of the trouble that would cause Wolfe to abandon the continuation of his proposed *Of Time and the River* series: Aline Bernstein had called on Perkins while Wolfe was abroad and told him that she would do everything in her power to prevent the publication of the new manuscript if she was portrayed as a character in it. According to Perkins, Wolfe "did not seem to take this too seriously, and asked me if that was all. And when I assured him it was, he said, 'Well, then, now we can have a good time.'"[17]

After his bags were checked at the Hotel Lexington, the jubilant Wolfe showed Perkins the Eighth Street loft where he had written so much of *Look Homeward, Angel*. That evening, Wolfe and Perkins were joined by their friend Belinda Jelliffe. The trio went to the top of the Radio City building and later the roof restaurant of the St. Moritz where they looked down upon the city. This happiness was recalled a month before Wolfe's death in the last letter he ever wrote.

Wolfe grudgingly abandoned Eugene and the beautiful Esther on the last pages of *Of Time and the River*, on the ocean liner where they had just met, as the ship was "given to the darkness and the sea."[18] He then began his next fictional project, which he called "The Hound of Darkness." It would be about nighttime in America. He wanted to present a series of scenes representative of American life taken simultaneously through the country on a single night. Wolfe never finished "The Hound of Darkness," but during the following three years he wrote large chunks of lyrical material for it that later found places in what became *The Web and the Rock* and *You Can't Go Home Again*. The essence of the proposed novel was embodied, however, in a short piece, also called "The Hound of Darkness," which appeared in the February 1, 1938, issue of *Vogue* (under the editor's title, "A Prologue to America").

From July 31 to August 7, Wolfe participated in the sixth annual Writers' Conference at Boulder, Colorado. (Robert Frost and Robert Penn Warren were among the participants.) Wolfe delivered a paper adapted from a long preface he had written for *Of Time and the River* that Perkins had persuaded him to excise. The talk was later revised and published in serial form in *The Saturday Review of Literature* and in book form by Scribner's on April 21, 1936, as *The Story of a Novel*.

The Boulder talk was an overwhelming success, and Wolfe continued on a vacation to the West Coast in the highest of spirits. He visited Hollywood where he briefly considered working as a screenwriter, and traveled to San Francisco, a city he had wanted to see since he heard of his father's adventures there. He returned east by way of St. Louis and visited the house where 12-year-old Grover died. He met its owner and pointed out the room where his brother died. This visit inspired his powerful novella *The Lost Boy*. Although Wolfe had described Grover's death in *Look Homeward, Angel*, he now gave the tragedy a more complete treatment.

Wolfe returned to New York the last week of September and, before settling down to work, began looking for a place to live in Manhattan. He had achieved what he set out to accomplish in Brooklyn and needed to learn more about New York City for his next book. On October 1 he moved into a three-room apartment on the 14th floor of 865 First Avenue, with a magnificent view of the East River. The apartment was only two blocks from the Perkinses' town house at Turtle Bay where he was always welcome and where he spent a large amount of his free time over the next two years.

On November 24 Scribner's published Wolfe's collection of short stories, *From Death to Morning*. The 14 stories were not favorably received and sold only 5,392 copies during the book's first year in print. However, by December 1935, *Of Time and the River* had sold 40,000 copies, and Thomas Wolfe was jubilant. He invited several of his old friends from Chapel Hill to a party at his new apartment on Christmas Eve. It was both a celebration of the success of *Of Time and the River* and a belated housewarming. Always sentimental about Christmas, Wolfe reached up to the ceiling of his living room and scrawled with a black crayon, "Merry Christmas to all my friends and love from Tom." As Elizabeth Nowell later remembered:

> The message stayed there on the ceiling for the two years that Wolfe lived at 865 First Avenue, and often, when he was pacing up and down, he'd glance up at it and smile. It was a symbol of his new-found happiness, his increasing freedom from the morbid supersensitivity of his own ego, and his greater love for all his fellow men.[19]

NOTES

1. *Letters*, 250.

2. *Ibid.*, 240.

3. *Notebooks*, II, 494.

4. *My Other Loneliness: Letters of Thomas Wolfe and Aline Bernstein*, Suzanne Stutman, ed. (Chapel Hill: University of North Carolina Press, 1983), 322.

5. *Ibid.*, 340–341.

6. Roy Wilder Jr., "Here Are Mother's Memories of Tom Wolfe," *Charlotte Observer*, October 29, 1950.

7. *The Letters of Thomas Wolfe to His Mother*, 192.

8. *Letters*, 279.

9. *Beyond Love and Loyalty: The Letters of Thomas Wolfe and Elizabeth Nowell*, Richard S. Kennedy, ed. (Chapel Hill: University of North Carolina Press, 1983), xxi.

10. *The Autobiography of an American Novelist*, 80.

11. *Letters*, 446.

12. *The Autobiography of an American Novelist*, 82.

13. *Letters*, 434.

14. *Ibid.*, 438.

15. *Ibid.*, 434.

16. *Ibid.*, 434.

17. Nowell, 279.

18. *Of Time and the River*, 912.

19. Nowell, 294.

5

"I Have a Thing to Tell You" and "Return" to Asheville 1936 – 1937

*And I have come back now; I have come home
again, and there is nothing more that I can say. —
All arguments are ended: saying nothing, all is
said then; all is known: I am home.*

—"Return"

Thomas Wolfe in front of the Yancey County
Courthouse, Burnsville, North Carolina, August
1937.

*Photo courtesy of The Thomas Wolfe Collection, Pack
Memorial Public Library, Asheville, North Carolina.*

N MARCH 17, 1936, while on a brief trip to Boston, Wolfe telegraphed Maxwell Perkins: "Wrote book beginning. Goes wonderfully. Full of hope."[1] He gave his new book the tentative title "The Vision of Spangler's Paul," and it later was consolidated into what became *The Web and the Rock* and *You Can't Go Home Again.* His hero's name, "Spangler," came from Spangler's Run, a stream that ran near his father's birthplace in Pennsylvania; "Paul" was adopted from the name of the Apostle. Wolfe considered using a quotation from The Acts of the Apostles on the title page: "And Paul said, I would to God that not only thou, but also all that hear me this day, were both almost, and altogether such as I am—except these bonds."[2] As a legend at the beginning of the new book, Wolfe also intended to use a quotation from *War and Peace:* "Prince Andrei . . . turned away. . . . His heart was heavy and full of melancholy. It was all so strange, so unlike what he had anticipated."[3]

Another great creative cycle had begun: one night soon after Wolfe plunged into "The Vision of Spangler's Paul," a neighbor of the Perkinses, Nancy Hale, at three or four o'clock in the morning, heard a deep chant growing louder and louder. She looked out the window and saw Wolfe marching down the deserted street with his tremendous stride, chanting, "I wrote ten thousand words today! I wrote ten thousand words today!"[4] Wolfe worked intermittently on "Spangler's Paul" for the next two years, his last creative cycle broken only by his death.

But soon came the beginning of the end: literary critic Bernard DeVoto published his infamous essay/review "Genius Is Not Enough" in the *Saturday Review of Literature* on April 25, 1936. Purportedly a review of the recently published *The Story of a Novel,* the article was an unwarranted and vicious attack on Thomas Wolfe. DeVoto's harsh criticisms plagued Wolfe the remaining two years of his life and contributed largely to his decision to leave Maxwell Perkins and Scribner's. DeVoto accused Wolfe of being "astonishingly immature"[5] as a novelist, offering the charge that Wolfe could not work without Perkins's help:

"The most flagrant evidence of his incompleteness is the fact that, so far, one indispensable part of the artist has existed not in Mr. Wolfe but in Maxwell Perkins. Such organizing faculty and such critical intelligence as have been applied to the book have come not from inside the artist, not from the artist's feeling for form and esthetic integrity, but from the office of Charles Scribner's Sons."[6]

Wolfe eventually came to the decision that he would have to leave Perkins and what DeVoto called "the assembly-line at Scribner's"[7] in order to prove he could write his books without anyone's help. But there were other reasons for Wolfe's final break. During the winter of 1935–1936, Wolfe had two quarrels with Perkins. The first was over his announcement that he wanted his royalties and advances in a bank account instead of being held in custody at Scribner's. (A bank account was soon established for him.) The second was over royalties from *The Story of a Novel*. The actual amount of money he was to receive from the book, he believed, had not been made clear.

Another reason for the breach was a series of legal difficulties and lawsuits in which Wolfe was involved and for which he was unfairly inclined to blame Perkins. The first suit had been brought by his agent for *Look Homeward, Angel*, Madeleine Boyd. Mrs. Boyd claimed that besides her commission for *Look Homeward, Angel*, she deserved a commission on Wolfe's other publications. The second was Aline Bernstein's threat of a lawsuit if "The October Fair" was published with a portrayal of her in it. Wolfe also unfairly blamed Perkins for exposing him to other libel suits, including one filed by the Dorman family from whom Wolfe had rented his apartment at 40 Verandah Place in Brooklyn. Marjorie Dorman and her family were suing for libel, claiming Wolfe had portrayed her as "Mad Maude" and depicted insanity in their family in "No Door." The fourth suit was one that Wolfe filed against a young manuscript dealer, Muredach J. Dooher, for withholding manuscripts Wolfe had given him to sell and later had demanded their unsuccessful return.

Still another cause for Wolfe's break was Perkins's opposition to Wolfe writing about the staff at Scribner's. Wolfe had long been fascinated by Scribner's and, during his many conversations with Perkins, his editor told him not only about the history of the firm, but details about the private lives of staff members. When Perkins discovered in the spring of 1936 that Wolfe had begun writing about a publishing house called "James Rodney & Sons," he realized his highly confidential and intimate details about his associates were in danger of being revealed. Perkins had little objection to being written about himself, but he felt— not altogether logically—that if Wolfe published anything derogatory about the staff, it would be his duty to resign.

Exhausted by the complexity of his problems with Perkins, Wolfe needed a vacation. *Of Time and the River* had been published in Germany in April and was a huge critical and commercial success. But because of Nazi restrictions against exporting money, he could not obtain his royalties unless he spent them in Germany. When a German magazine, the *Seven Seas*, offered him $150 worth of free passage on the *Europa* in exchange for an article or two about Germany, he could not resist the temptation. He boarded the *Europa* on July 23, 1936, for his seventh and last trip to Europe.

Wolfe went straight to Berlin. During the previous year in Germany, he had been too busy enjoying his fame to acknowledge the problems of Hitler's regime, but he now detected increasing terrorism and could no longer ignore the atmosphere. This year, as his friend Ambassador William Dodd remarked, "only the horses seemed happy"[8] in Germany.

The previous year, Wolfe had heard "some ugly things" but "I did not see anyone beaten, I did not see anyone imprisoned, or put to death, I did not see any of the men in concentration camps, I did not see openly anywhere the physical manifestations of a brutal and compulsive force."[9] Nevertheless, in 1936, despite an even greater welcome, he could not ignore an unmistakable darker side: "It was the season of the great Olympic

Games," he wrote, "and every day I went to the stadium in Berlin. And, just as that year of absence had marked the evidence of a cruel and progressive dissolution in the lives of all the people I had known, so had it also marked the overwhelming evidence of an increased concentration, a stupendous organization, a tremendous drawing together and ordering, in the vast collective power of the whole land."[10]

Outside the stadium the spectacle was overwhelming. Wolfe witnessed enormous masses waiting for the arrival of their leader—the "Dark Messiah"—as Wolfe dubbed Hitler. Ambassador Dodd's daughter, Martha, told of the afternoon that Wolfe sat with her in the diplomatic box. When American athlete Jesse Owens "won a particularly conspicuous victory, Tom let out a war whoop," she recorded in a book of reminiscences. "Hitler twisted in his seat, looked down, attempting to locate the miscreant, and frowned angrily."[11] Miss Dodd explained it was the Nazi attitude that Negroes were unqualified to enter the Olympic games.

Thea Voelcker's "Schweinsgesicht" drawing of Thomas Wolfe, which accompanied an interview in the August 5, 1936, issue of the *Berliner Tageblatt.*

Photo courtesy of the Aldo P. Magi Collection.

Shortly before the Olympics began, Wolfe fell in love with tall, blond Thea Voelcker, who had been assigned by a German newspaper, the *Berliner Tageblatt,* to do a drawing of him to accompany an interview. When the drawing was published, he was offended by the caricature, complaining it gave him a "Schweinsgesicht" (swine's face). Eventually his anger abated, and a brief but tempestuous love affair began. The affair ended after quarrels during a trip in the Austrian Tirol. However, they continued to correspond after Wolfe returned to New York. "Else von Kohler" in *You Can't Go Home Again* is based on Thea Voelcker.

On September 8 Wolfe left Berlin by train for Paris. At the border, crossing into Belgium at Aachen, he witnessed the arrest of a fellow passenger, a nondescript Jewish clerk. The bullying of the clerk by the Nazis inspired Wolfe's novella "I Have a Thing to Tell You," which was posthumously enlarged and consolidated into *You Can't Go Home Again*. He began writing of the clerk's brutalization in Paris, telling Elizabeth Nowell on September 16, "I've written a good piece over here—I'm afraid it may mean that I can't come back to the place where I am liked best and have the most friends, but I've decided to publish it."[12] He was warned by his German publisher not to publish the novella or his works would be banned in Germany. Although Wolfe himself tended toward anti-Semitism acquired during his youth, this border arrest made him realize that not only was the Jewish clerk being brutalized, but all of humanity. The revelation marked a new maturity for Thomas Wolfe:

> He lifted his eyes to us, his pasty face, and he was silent for a moment. And we looked at him for the last time, and he at us—this time, more direct and steadfastly. And in that glance there was all the silence of man's mortal anguish. And we were all somehow naked and ashamed, and somehow guilty. We all felt somehow that we were saying farewell, not to a man but to humanity; not to some nameless little cipher out of life, but to the fading image of a brother's face.[13]

"I Have a Thing to Tell You" was published in three install-ments in the *New Republic* in 1937, and consequently, Wolfe's works were banned in Germany for the duration of Hitler's regime. As much as Wolfe loved Germany, after "I Have a Thing to Tell You," he could never go back. As soon as he returned to New York, he wrote to the *Seven Seas* and asked them to release him from his promise. He returned the check for $150, which they had credited against the cost of his passage.

By October 1936 Wolfe's conviction that he would have to leave Scribner's was increased by Perkins's unfavorable reaction to Wolfe's recent short story "No More Rivers." The major difficulty was that Wolfe portrayed Scribner's editor, Wallace Meyer, as an easily recognized character. Wolfe also included satirical vignettes that reflected upon other members of the firm. Perkins and Elizabeth Nowell convinced Wolfe to revise the story (although it was not published during his lifetime), but from that time forth, Wolfe began avoiding stopping by Scribner's to see Perkins and pick up his mail, instead having it forwarded to his First Avenue apartment. Wolfe drafted a formal letter of release, stating he had discharged all of his obligations to Scribner's and was no longer under contract to them.

The severance from Scribner's was not quite complete when Wolfe left to go to New Orleans for New Year's and for a much needed vacation. (His longer statements of severance were packed in his suitcase when he left New York in late December.) He arrived in New Orleans on January 1, 1937. It took only a day or two for the news to get around that Thomas Wolfe was in town, and he was soon engulfed by fans and friends. The most important event of his excursion was meeting advertising man and bibliophile William B. Wisdom, a great admirer of Wolfe's writing. After Wolfe's death, Wisdom purchased Wolfe's manuscripts and personal papers and donated them to Harvard University.

Leaving New Orleans on January 11, Wolfe stopped in Biloxi, Mississippi, for a rest before going on to Atlanta. From Atlanta he returned to North Carolina for the first time in seven years. But because of confusion with his brother Fred during a telephone conversation, he did not disembark when the train stopped in Asheville. Wolfe had indicated to Fred that he wanted to return to Asheville. But when Fred suggested he meet Tom in Spartanburg, South Carolina, instead of coming directly to Asheville, Tom thought his family did not want him to come home. Julia Wolfe later claimed that Tom kept saying repeatedly over the phone, "Are you ashamed of me? Don't you want to see me? Are you ashamed of me?"[14] Tom soon wrote Fred, "I should have liked to come to Asheville and intended to do so, but when I called you up from Atlanta there seemed to be some excitement and confusion about my coming, or whether I wanted to come or not, so I was too tired to argue the point and decided to pass my visit up until some other time."[15]

Wolfe then visited Southern Pines where he stayed with author James Boyd. After a night in Raleigh, he spent several days in Chapel Hill at the University of North Carolina, enjoying a warm reunion with faculty and friends. But once back in New York, he soon found himself embroiled in more difficulties with Scribner's. He had mailed one letter of severance from New Orleans even though Maxwell Perkins had attempted to convince him that Scribner's was still interested in publishing him. Wolfe did not entirely relinquish his friendship with Perkins and saw him on occasion socially. He continued to sit for a portrait by Perkins's son-in-law, Douglas Gorsline, all the while expressing his grievances against Scribner's and Perkins. Finally, during one of their quarrels, an exasperated Perkins declared, "All right then, if you *must* leave Scribner's, go ahead and *leave*, but for heaven's sake, *don't talk about it any more!*"[16] Later, Wolfe's resentment became so heated that the two men came close to actual blows. Fortunately, Wolfe's attention was diverted by a tall, attractive woman who threw her arms around him and said, "This is what I came to New York to see!"[17]

In March Wolfe was ill with influenza for a week. When his fever persisted, he went to a physician. Neither the identity of the physician nor his actual diagnosis has been discovered. However, Elizabeth Nowell has reported that X rays were taken of Wolfe's lungs at this time and revealed an old tubercular scar on his right upper lobe. Wolfe told Miss Nowell he had been to a physician and "there's something the matter with my lung,"[18] but refused to talk about it. Despite this intimation of mortality (Wolfe had long had a terror of tuberculosis), he worked hard from February to the spring of 1937 on "The Vision of Spangler's Paul" as well as a number of short stories.

By April Wolfe was ready for another vacation and decided to set out on his long-anticipated return to Asheville. He made his journey in short stages, first visiting his father's home, York Springs, Pennsylvania, where in Latimore, he copied inscriptions from gravestones in Gardner's Church cemetery. He journeyed down the Shenandoah Valley, stopping in Roanoke, where he purchased a copy of *Gone with the Wind* (which he called an "immortal piece of bilge"[19]). He was "loafing"[20] and in no hurry to reach Asheville: "I am dreading Asheville a little," he wrote Elizabeth Nowell from Roanoke on April 28, "but I think I will be ready for it in a few days."[21]

Wolfe arrived in Bristol, near the Tennessee-Virginia state line on Thursday, April 29, and registered at the General Shelby Hotel. Several Bristolians visited him in his hotel room. "One has to go away," he told a reporter from the *Bristol News*, "before he learns how deeply he is attached to his own people and own country."[22] He met novelist Anne W. Armstrong, who offered him a secluded cabin on her property so he could write in peace that summer. Wolfe declined the invitation but considered it for future use. He departed the following evening, Friday the 30th, and stopped in Yancey County, North Carolina, for a few days to look up Westall relatives.

Wolfe registered at the Nu-Wray Inn in Burnsville and placed a call from a phone booth in the lobby to his family to determine if it was "safe" to return to Asheville. Once settled, he began making inquiries about his mother's family and encountered everywhere people who claimed to be relatives. "Everybody's kinfolks here,"[23] he soon found out.

On Saturday night, May 1, between 10:30 and 11:00, Wolfe stepped out of the Gem City Soda Shop on Main Street in Burnsville and into an altercation between Otis Chase, Philip Ray, and James O. Higgins. When Wolfe saw Ray pull out a pistol to fire at Higgins, "I got behind an automobile and after that some shots were fired but I did not see who fired the shots," Wolfe later testified at the trial held that August. "I couldn't say definitely how many shots were fired but I would say three or four. I heard a bullet hit two tires, or at any rate you could hear the sound of air going out of the tires. I don't know that a bullet hit one of the tires on the automobile I was behind, but it was either that one or the one next to me."[24] Although none of the feuders were killed that night, a week later, on May 8, when Ray and Higgins met again on the same spot as the previous shooting, Ray shot and killed Higgins. Wolfe was later subpoenaed to testify as a witness to the earlier altercation.

Before leaving Burnsville, Wolfe visited his great-half-uncle, John B. Westall, on the South Toe River, and listened to his reminiscences of the Civil War battle at Chickamauga. When Wolfe returned to New York, he fictionalized his great-uncle's reminiscences into "Chickamauga," which he rightfully considered one of his best short stories.

Wolfe arrived in Asheville on Monday, May 3. From the bus station, he took a taxi to the Old Kentucky Home, where, in short order, he and his mother were photographed on the porch of the shabby, gaunt house. For days the telephone rang as well-wishers and friends called to welcome him home. At one time, there were as many as six people waiting to see him. During the next few days, Wolfe walked through Asheville, visiting many old and familiar places. He went to see his birthplace at 92 Woodfin Street and followed one of the paper routes he once carried. But he made little apology for *Look Homeward, Angel.* "If anything I have ever written has displeased anyone in Asheville, I hope that I will be able to write another book which will please them,"[25] he told a reporter for the *Asheville Citizen.*

Wolfe rented a cabin from cartoonist Max Whitson in nearby Oteen, planning to work all summer in it, hoping for seclusion. He later wrote his brother Fred, "I don't think anybody quite understood when I was home just how tired I am and how much I need now a period of quiet and seclusion. But I do need it very

LEE COUNTY LIBRARY
107 Hawkins Ave.
Sanford, NC 27330

Thomas Wolfe and his mother Julia on the porch of the Old Kentucky Home, May 1937. One of Wolfe's objectives for making the trip to Asheville was to see if he could help his mother untangle her financial troubles with Wachovia Bank. Mrs. Wolfe speculated wildly on real estate during the '20s, and after the stock market crashed in 1929, she found she had over-speculated and could no longer pay her mortgages or taxes. Wachovia Bank was now suing her for the foreclosure of deeds of trust she had executed to secure payments.

Photo by Elliot Lyman Fisher; courtesy of The Thomas Wolfe Collection, Pack Memorial Public Library, Asheville, North Carolina.

badly, and that is the reason that I have taken the little cabin out near Asheville in the hope and belief that I can get it there."[26]

Wolfe's self-imposed "exile" had ended in triumphant victory, although not to the extent of his fictional rendering of the event: "The only ones who are mad today are those you left out!"[27] Although most of the feathers Wolfe ruffled in 1929 had been smoothed out, many of the victims of *Look Homeward, Angel* were slow to forget or forgive what Wolfe had written about them and their families. As late as 1938, many Ashevillians were still not ready to bury the hatchet even when Thomas Wolfe was buried.

Before leaving on May 15 for New York, Wolfe was asked by his friend George W. McCoy, a journalist for the *Asheville Citizen*, to write an article about his feelings at being home again. Wolfe readily agreed, and the evocative prose-poem "Return" appeared in the May 16, 1937, issue of the *Citizen*.

Wolfe returned to New York for six weeks to prepare material for Elizabeth Nowell to sell to magazines as well as to pack his manuscripts for his stay in Oteen. "I am bringing a great amount of manuscript with me and shall work on it this summer,"[28] he wrote his mother. His main concern was his massive work-in-progress. "There is an immense amount of it, millions of words, and although it might not be of any use to anyone else, it is, so far as I am concerned, the most valuable thing I have got,"[29] he wrote Fred Wolfe on June 26.

Leaving New York on July 1 and arriving at the Biltmore station outside of Asheville the next day, Wolfe went directly to the Oteen cabin. On the afternoon of July 10 a photographer hired by the *Asheville Citizen-Times* paid a visit to the cabin and found Wolfe with his shirt sleeves rolled up, tie discarded and collar open, writing longhand. Wolfe explained that his new book would be "a chronicle to the modern Gulliver."[30] He hired a black man called Ed to cook and help with the chores at the

cabin. Ed was an excellent cook but was usually intoxicated and could never remember Wolfe's last name, often calling him "Mr. Fox."

There were several reunions with his family in Asheville and at the cabin. Friends and curiosity seekers flocked to Oteen, and Wolfe wrote to a correspondent, "It's pretty hard to tell you what I shall do about staying here in Asheville. I wanted to come back: I thought about it for years. . . . But my stay here this summer has really resembled a three-ring circus. I think people have wanted

Thomas Wolfe in his cabin at Oteen, summer 1937.

Photo by W. Frank Clodfelter; courtesy of the North Carolina Department of Cultural Resources.

Judge Philip Cocke, Thomas Wolfe, and an unidentified woman in front of the Oteen cabin, July 1937. Wolfe accomplished little in the cabin except the third draft of "The Party at Jack's." This novella was about a fire that disrupted a party at Aline Bernstein's apartment at 270 Park Avenue, at which artist Alexander Calder entertained the guests with a circus of mechanical animals and dolls. "The Party at Jack's" would render Wolfe's growing sense of social injustice by contrasting the harsh realities of the working class and the luxury of the more privileged class.

Photo by permission of the Houghton Library, Harvard University, and the Estate of Thomas Wolfe.

to be and have tried to be most kind, but they wore me to a frazzle. My cabin outside of town was situated in an isolated and quite beautiful spot, but they found their way to it. . . ."[31]

The first week of August, a Buncombe County deputy sheriff located Wolfe in Oteen and served him with a subpoena to appear on August 16 in Burnsville as a state's witness to the shooting he witnessed in May. Wolfe went to Burnsville on the 16th and spent the night at the Nu-Wray Inn. He testified on the 17th. By the time the trial was completed on the 20th, his testimony had been discredited by one of the defense attorneys. He wrote Hamilton Basso on August 21:

> I had to attend a murder trial in Yancey and testify. It was
> a fascinating and thrilling and exhausting experience. I got off
> fairly lightly compared to some of the witnesses, but I was

denounced by one of the defense lawyers in his final plea to the jury as the author of an obscene and infamous book called "Look Homeward, Angel," who had held up his family, kin-folk, and town to public odium, and whose testimony, I therefore gathered, was not to be taken into account.[32]

After the trial, Wolfe returned to Asheville and got roaring drunk. The pressures of the trial as well as his growing dissatisfaction with Asheville had pushed him over the edge. "Do you wonder that sometimes this past summer I went berserk?"[33] he later asked Anne W. Armstrong. It took two officers to subdue him, and he spent the night in the city jail. He was released the following morning after he sobered up, and no charges were filed. There is little wonder that he wrote Margaret Roberts, "A prophet may be without honor in his own country, but he is also without privacy."[34] The prodigal's victorious return was, for all intents and purposes, brought to an abrupt conclusion.

Soon after his day in court, Wolfe left the Oteen cabin and moved into the Battery Park Hotel in downtown Asheville. He gave his secretary strict instructions not to reveal his whereabouts to anyone—including his mother. There had been too many disturbing contacts with his family that summer and he needed to work in undisturbed peace and quiet. With more privacy than the cabin afforded him, he finished the third draft of "The Party at Jack's," but he was now more depressed than ever and drinking heavily. He later claimed he was as near to a breakdown as he had ever been.

One of the last things Wolfe did before leaving Asheville was to visit his friend J. Y. Jordan at his office six floors high in the Jackson Building in the city square. Wolfe looked out the window, gazing at the hills and mountains encircling the city, as though he would never again set eyes on them. He left on September 2, carrying under his arm the 80,000-word manuscript he had written since July, "The Party at Jack's."

Wolfe stopped for several days in Bristol, Tennessee, relaxing in the cabin Anne W. Armstrong had offered him. At the end of the visit, Mrs. Armstrong drove him to Marion, Virginia, where he spent two days with novelist Sherwood Anderson, one of his literary idols. Before returning to New York, Wolfe stopped at Baltimore and recounted his woes to newspaper editor R.P. Harriss of the *Baltimore Evening Sun*: "I've been down home at Asheville, and I found that being forgiven was almost worse than being damned. Did you ever have just too much hospitality?"[35]

After giving up his First Avenue apartment, Wolfe moved to various hotels, finally settling at the Hotel Chelsea at 222 W. 23rd Street. He rented room 829, a two-room suite with an anteroom for his typist. He stayed alone much of the time and communicated with almost no one except Elizabeth Nowell. He kept his whereabouts a secret, even from his family. His break with Scribner's now became publicly known. Before leaving Asheville, he had called several publishers asking whether they would be interested in publishing his future novels. "My name is Wolfe," he would blurt out, often intoxicated. "Would you like to publish me?"[36] Some thought it a joke, others were concerned about his leaving Scribner's. His search for a publisher would continue for the remainder of the year. As the weeks went by, he grew convinced that no publisher wanted him. His troubles with Scribner's were "deep, grievous, and I fear, irreparable."[37]

On December 1 Wolfe attended a dinner at socialite Mary Emmet's for the Sherwood Andersons. Also attending the party was Ella Winter, the widow of Lincoln Steffens. When the party was over, Wolfe walked Ella Winter home, pouring out his grievances against Perkins as well as what he had found on his trip to Asheville. As Miss Winter recalled, "He started telling me about his horror at going back to his home and what he found there, and I just said, 'But don't you know you can't go home again?' He stopped dead and then said: 'Can I have that? I mean for a title? I'm writing a piece . . . and I'd like to call it that. It says exactly what I mean. Would you mind if I used it?' I laughed and told him that I didn't 'own' it any more than I'd own any other thought."[38] From that time on, Wolfe became obsessed with the phrase "You can't go home again." He proclaimed it to friends as a revolutionizing discovery and chanted it over and over to himself. Recognizing the importance of the phrase to almost every aspect of his life and work, he began to consider it as a title for his work in progress.

. . . the whole book might almost be called "You Can't Go Home Again"—which means back home to one's family, back home to one's childhood, back home to the father one has lost, back home to romantic love, to a young man's dreams of glory and of fame, back home to exile, to escape to "Europe" and some foreign land, back home to lyricism, singing just for singing's sake, back home to aestheticism, to one's youthful ideas of the "artist," and the all-sufficiency of "art and beauty and love," back home to the ivory tower, back home to places in the country, the cottage in Bermuda away from all the strife and conflict of the world, back home to the father one is looking for—to someone who can help one, save one, ease the burden for one, back home to the old forms and systems of things that once seemed everlasting, but that are changing all the time—back home to the escapes of Time and Memory. Each of these discoveries, sad and hard as they are to make and accept, are described in the book almost in the order in which they are named here. But the conclusion is not sad: this is a hopeful book—the conclusion is that although you can't go home again, the home of every one of us is in the future: there is no other way.

—*The Letters of Thomas Wolfe*, 711–712

Edward C. Aswell. "I will be associated with a young man just exactly my own age, who is second in command," Thomas Wolfe wrote of Aswell. "I think it is going to turn out to be a wonderful experience—I feel that the man is quiet, but very deep and true: and he thinks that I am the best writer there is. I know he is wrong about this, but if anyone feels that way, you are going to do your utmost to try to live up to it, aren't you?" (*Letters*, 695.)

Photo by Fabian Bachrach; courtesy of Dr. Mary Aswell Doll.

Wolfe negotiated with various publishers, finally settling on Harper & Brothers. He was elated by his new editor, Edward C. Aswell, a fellow southerner from Tennessee, also a Harvard graduate, and six days younger than Wolfe.

Wolfe spent Christmas with Edward and Mary Louise Aswell and their infant son Edward Duncan in Chappaqua, outside of New York. There were a dozen people at the party. "We really did have a swell Christmas out at Ed Aswell's—I think it was the best one I have had since I was a kid," Wolfe wrote Elizabeth Nowell on December 29. As they finished dinner, Mrs. Aswell whispered to Wolfe asking if it would be all right to announce that Harper's was to be his publishers. He readily agreed. "So we got out your bottle of champagne and Mary Lou told them," he wrote Miss Nowell, "and I tried to say something and Ed tried to say something, and neither could very well, and everyone had tears in their eyes, and I think they meant it, too."[39]

On December 31 Wolfe signed a $10,000 contract with Harper's for a novel, "The Life and Adventures of the Bondsman

Doaks." He received an advance of $2,500 on that day, with the balance to be paid in three installments of $2,500 each on February 1, March 1, and April 1, 1938. After signing the contract, he wrote Mary Louise Aswell, "The final grim technical details of business and contract signing have been attended to, and now I am committed utterly, in every way. It gives me a strangely empty and hollow feeling, and I know the importance of the moment, and feel more than ever the responsibility of the obligation I have assumed." Then, on the last day of a particularly momentous year, he added:

> But I guess it is good for a man to get that hollow empty feeling, the sense of absolute loneliness and new beginning at different times throughout his life. It's not the hollowness of death, but a living kind of hollowness: a new world is before me now; it's good to know I have your prayers.[40]

NOTES

1. *Letters*, 496.

2. Acts 26:29.

3. *Letters*, 527.

4. Nowell, 300.

5. C. Hugh Holman, *The World of Thomas Wolfe* (New York: Charles Scribner's Sons, 1962), 88.

6. *Ibid.*, 88.

7. *Ibid.*, 89.

8. *Notebooks*, II, 822.

9. *Ibid.*, pp. 905–906.

10. *Ibid.*, 911.

11. Martha Dodd, *Through Embassy Eyes* (New York: Harcourt, Brace and Company, 1939), 212.

12. *Letters*, 541.

13. *The Short Novels of Thomas Wolfe*, C. Hugh Holman, ed. (New York: Charles Scribner's Sons, 1961), 274.

14. *Raleigh News & Observer*, October 29, 1950.

15. *Letters*, 609.

16. Nowell, 375.

17. *Ibid.*, 377.

18. *Ibid.*, 378.

19. *Letters*, 747.

20. *Ibid.*, 615.

21. *Beyond Love and Loyalty*, 57.

22. *Bristol News*, April 30, 1937.

23. *The Complete Short Stories of Thomas Wolfe*, Francis E. Skipp, ed. (New York: Charles Scribner's Sons, 1987), 552.

24. No. 146, Eighteenth District, Supreme Court of North Carolina, Fall Term, 1937, State v. Philip Ray and Otis Chase, Record on Appeal, 20. Note: Wolfe's words here are not necessarily verbatim, but an approximation of his testimony.

25. *Asheville Citizen*, May 4, 1937.

26. *Letters*, 621.

27. *Complete Short Stories*, 556.

28. *The Letters of Thomas Wolfe to His Mother*, 282.

29. *Letters*, 619.

30. *Asheville Citizen-Times*, July 11, 1937.

31. *Letters*, 653.

32. *Ibid.*, 650.

33. Anne W. Armstrong, "As I Saw Thomas Wolfe," *Arizona Quarterly* 2:1 (Spring 1946): 8.

34. *Letters*, 740.

35. R.P. Harriss, "A Memoir of Thomas Wolfe," *Baltimore Evening Sun*, September 16, 1938.

36. Nowell, 392.

37. *Letters*, 655.

38. Nowell, 410.

39. *Letters*, 696.

40. *Ibid.*, 698.

6

The Last Voyage, the Longest, the Best
1938

Live a little now, I entreat you; for we are as the men of former time—no different, and in the end we, too, shall turn our faces to the wall, and the light will go out; and we shall go into a place where there is darkness,—nothing but darkness.
—*The Letters of Thomas Wolfe to His Mother,* 60

The last clear photo of Thomas Wolfe; July 4, 1938, Seattle, Washington, two days before the onset of his fatal illness.

Photo courtesy of The North Carolina Collection, University of North Carolina Library at Chapel Hill, and the Estate of Thomas Wolfe.

T THE BEGINNING of 1938, Wolfe launched into intensive work on his new novel. During his visit to Asheville in 1937, he decided to write about the scandal surrounding the failure of the Central Bank and Trust Company. He began devising ways his huge "October Fair" manuscript could be consolidated into his "Bondsman Doaks" book. He hired a typist, Gwen Jassinoff, and dictated material to her as she typed. He began assembling new and old material that would take Doaks through the Depression in both "Libya Hill" (his new fictional counterpart for Asheville) and New York. He wrote Aswell that he had decided to consolidate the material he had written for "The October Fair," "Spangler's Paul," and "Bondsman Doaks" into a complete biographical chronicle. He chose a new title, "The Web and the Rock," as well as a new name, George Webber, for his protagonist. "Let his name be Webber,"[1] he jotted down in his notes for the manuscript.

On March 31 Professor F. A. Cummings of the Department of English at Purdue University wired Wolfe, asking him to speak at the annual Literary Awards Banquet at Purdue on May 19, in West Lafayette, Indiana. Wolfe was pleased with the honorarium of $300 and accepted the offer. He decided to make Purdue the first stop on his second trip to the West, planning to travel through the Northwest to soak up local color.

By May 9 Wolfe had given large sections of his manuscript to Elizabeth Nowell to read. Miss Nowell persuaded Wolfe to allow Edward Aswell to familiarize himself with the manuscript. Just before Wolfe left for Purdue on the evening of May 17, Aswell arrived at Wolfe's suite at the Hotel Chelsea to collect the massive manuscript and found Wolfe still busy sorting it out.

Gwen Jassinoff and Wolfe had already prepared a long outline to help identify the manuscript that comprised the two huge bundles Aswell later left with under his arms. The manuscript totaled more than 4,000 typewritten pages and contained over 1,200,000 words. When Aswell later prepared it for posthumous publication (as three volumes, *The Web and the Rock, You*

Can't Go Home Again, and *The Hills Beyond*), he used only the enormous bundles he had taken from Wolfe. The three large wooden packing crates full of material Wolfe had acquired since he first began writing had been turned over to his executor, Maxwell Perkins, soon after Wolfe's death. Wolfe all-too-accurately described himself as "a vagabond writer with two tons of manuscript."[2]

Wolfe boarded the train on May 17 at 9 P.M. After the talk at Purdue and a vacation through the West, he planned to return to New York and locate a place out of town to spend the summer and keep on with his work. However, he was never to return to work on his massive manuscript. He had worked furiously the last three years with the half-repressed fear that he would die before he accomplished the work he had set out to do. "His enemy was Time," he wrote of George Webber. "Or perhaps it was his friend. One never knows for sure."[3]

Wolfe's Purdue speech, "Writing and Living," was a triumph. He gave a well-prepared account of his career and revelations of his developing social consciousness. With several teachers and their wives, he rode to Chicago, spending "two very pleasant days together, eating, drinking, driving all over Chicago."[4] After this relaxing weekend, he boarded the *Burlington Zephyr* for Denver. There he had a reunion with friends he had met in

Thomas Wolfe, ca. 1937–1938. According to Gwen Jassinoff, Wolfe's typist in 1938, the photograph was taken at the Hotel Chelsea.

Photo courtesy of Clara Stites.

1935 at the Writers' Conference in Boulder. His friends did everything they could to show him a good time and Wolfe enjoyed himself so thoroughly that he extended his visit from one day to a week.

After brief stopovers in Cheyenne and Boise, Wolfe arrived in Portland on June 8. He was invited to join an experiment in tourism by Edward Miller, Sunday editor of the *Portland Oregonian*, and Ray Conway, an executive in the Oregon State Motor Association. Miller and Conway asked Wolfe to be their literary passenger as they toured 11 national parks by auto in a two-week period. The excursion was meant to prove that all of the

Thomas Wolfe with his traveling companions, Ray Conway and Ed Miller, Logan Pass, Glacier National Park, June 29, 1938. Wolfe described his itinerary to Elizabeth Nowell:

> We leave here Sunday and head south for California stopping at Crater Lake on the way down; we go down the whole length of California taking in Yosemite, the Sequoias and any other national parks they have; then we swing east across the desert into Arizona to the Grand Canyon, etc., north through Utah, Zion and Bryce Canyons, Salt Lake, etc., then to the Yellowstone, then North to the Canadian Border, Montana, Glacier Park, etc., then west again across Montana, Idaho, Washington, then Rainier Park, etc.—in other words a complete swing around the West from the Rocky Mountains on, and every big national park in the West.
>
> —*The Letters of Thomas Wolfe, 769.*

Photo courtesy of The Thomas Wolfe Collection, Pack Memorial Public Library, Asheville, North Carolina.

Western national parks could be visited within an average two-week vacation. The trip was conceived for travel promotion and proved to be a grueling drive. Wolfe eagerly accepted the invitation, believing it an excellent opportunity to absorb the West. "The West is the American horizon,"[5] he told Edward Miller.

The excursion began on June 20 at 8:15 A.M., leaving Portland for Crater Lake. For 13 days and 12 nights Wolfe and his companions traveled in a white Ford conspicuously displaying "Oregon State Motor Association" on its sides and trunk. Miller and Conway took turns driving (Wolfe had never learned to drive), while Wolfe sprawled out in the back seat. He kept a record of his impressions in a 6″ by 9″ ledger, doing most of his writing at night in lodges. By the time their journey ended at Mount Rainier on July 2, Wolfe had witnessed "the pity, terror, strangeness, and magnificence of it all."[6] Wolfe and his companions drove into Olympia, where they had lunch and a sentimental parting. Miller and Conway gave him the maps and old tour book they had worn black, and wrote their names in it. They had traveled 4,632 miles. That afternoon Wolfe caught a bus for Seattle.

Upon registering at the New Washington Hotel in Seattle, Wolfe received a wire from Edward Aswell: "Dear Tom: Your new book is magnificent in scope and design, with some of the best writing you have ever done. I am still absorbing it, confident that when you finish you will have written your greatest novel so far. Hope you come back full of health and new visions."[7]

On July 4 Wolfe watched an Independence Day parade with James and Theresa Stevens. Stevens, well-known in Seattle literary circles, was the compiler of Paul Bunyan stories and had met Wolfe during a short visit to Seattle Wolfe had made in June. After the parade, Wolfe and the Stevenses drove to the home of Ivar and Margaret Haglund in Alki, one of the oldest sections of Seattle. Three photographs taken of Wolfe that afternoon were the last clear photos made of him.

On July 5 Wolfe left for Victoria and Vancouver in British Columbia. He planned to be gone for a day or two and was eager to return and have his "Western Journal" typed. Sometime during this trip on the coastal steamer *Princess Kathleen*, he shared a pint of whiskey with a "poor, shivering wretch,"[8] and contracted a respiratory infection that soon activated the dormant tuberculosis in his right lung. On the afternoon of July 6 he began experiencing chills, pain in his lungs, and a high fever. He left Vancouver by train and returned to Seattle, remaining in the New Washington Hotel for five days before seeking treatment.

In June James Stevens and his wife had given a party to introduce Wolfe to some of the literary people of Seattle, and now Sophus Winther of the University of Washington asked Wolfe to a party in return. When the evening of the party, July 9, arrived, Wolfe was ill, but because he was the guest of honor, he felt he had to make an appearance. He arrived at 10 o'clock, wild-looking with a severe cold; no one realized how dangerously ill he was. Two days later, Wolfe phoned Theresa Stevens and asked her for the Winthers' phone number, telling her his cough was much worse and Mrs. Winther had promised to give him a cough remedy. Mrs. Stevens told him he didn't need a cough remedy—he needed a doctor. She persuaded him to see their family physician, Dr. E.C. Ruge. Dr. Ruge found Wolfe was suffering with a hacking cough and a fever of 102, and diagnosed pneumonia.

Dr. Ruge told Wolfe he needed hospitalization, but Wolfe dreaded hospitals. Dr. Ruge, a well-known general surgeon, diagnostician, and psychiatrist, had established a private sanatorium, Firlawns, 12 miles from Seattle at Kenmore. Wolfe agreed to be admitted there rather than at a big Seattle hospital. Although desperately ill, he managed to maintain his sense of humor: "They haven't yet made up their minds whether I'm Jesus Christ or Napoleon,"[9] he told a visitor after observing Dr. Ruge's mental patients. However, at Firlawns, Wolfe received the intensive care he needed. By July 14 the crisis seemed to have passed and his fever, which once reached 105, now dropped to 100. "Doctors say I'm out of danger now," Wolfe wired Edward Aswell on July 15. "Will write when I feel stronger."[10]

When Wolfe continued to have recurrent fevers, Dr. Ruge wired Wolfe's brother Fred to come. When Wolfe seemed unable to make a complete recovery, Dr. Ruge sent him to Providence Hospital in Seattle the first week of August so X rays could be made of his lungs. The X rays revealed a consolidation of the upper lobe of the right lung, which Dr. Ruge and the X-ray specialist at Providence diagnosed as an old tubercular lesion. When violent headaches and periods of irrationality began, the doctors suspected a brain tumor or abscess.

Wolfe remained at Providence under the care of Dr. Charles E. Watts after Fred Wolfe dismissed Dr. Ruge. Thomas Wolfe had been terrified of tuberculosis since his boyhood and did not want to hear, as he did from Dr. Ruge, that he was now one of the dreaded lungers. Dr. Watts diagnosed pneumonia, not tuberculosis, and Wolfe felt safer with the less ominous diagnosis. On August 12 Wolfe's fever shot up to 103. As his situation became desperate, he was uplifted by a warm letter from Maxwell Perkins. Overcome with longing for their old friendship, Wolfe insisted upon sitting up in bed and writing an immediate reply. (The text of this letter to Maxwell Perkins—the last letter Wolfe ever wrote—is reprinted on page 92.)

Wolfe's sister Mabel arrived in Seattle on August 19 to relieve Fred, who needed to return to his job. When Mabel appeared in his room, Wolfe blurted out, "Well, what do you think? Have you come out here to tell me I'm going to die?" When Mabel tried to reassure her brother, he said, "I have these headaches, Mabel, awful headaches."[11] His headaches increased in severity, and dilaudid had to be administered so he could sleep.

Wolfe believed if he could leave the hospital he would improve and decided to rent an apartment with Mabel for a week or two before going on to Dr. Russel Lee's clinic at Palo Alto to complete his convalescence. He asked Mabel to rent an apartment at the Spring Hotel Apartments he had admired before his illness because of its magnificent view of Puget Sound. On September 4 Mabel packed her brother's bags and paid his bill,

Maxwell Perkins.

Photo courtesy of The Thomas Wolfe Collection, Pack Memorial Public Library, Asheville, North Carolina.

Aug 12, 1938

Dear Max: I'm sneaking this against orders—but "I've got a hunch"—and I wanted to write these words to you.

—I've made a long voyage and been to a strange country, and I've seen the dark man very close; and I don't think I was too much afraid of him, but so much of mortality still clings to me—I wanted most desperately to live and still do, and I thought about you all a 1000 times, and wanted to see you all again, and there was the impossible anguish and regret of all the work I had not done, of all the work I had to do—and I know now I'm just a grain of dust, and I feel as if a great window has been opened on life I did not know about before—and if I come through this, I hope to God I am a better man, and in some strange way I can't explain I know I am a deeper and a wiser one—If I get on my feet and out of here, it will be months before I head back, but if I get on my feet, I'll come back.

—Whatever happens—I had this "hunch" and wanted to write you and tell you, no matter what happens or has happened, I shall always think of you and feel about you the way it was that 4th of July day 3 yrs. ago when you met me at the boat, and we went out on the café on the river and had a drink and later went on top of the tall building and all the strangeness and the glory and the power of life and of the city were below—

Yours Always

Tom

—Harvard Library Bulletin (Autumn 1947): 278

eager for his release. But before Wolfe was released, Dr. Watts conferred with her: "Mrs. Wheaton, I want to talk to you. You know this has not been any ordinary case of pneumonia. I've just looked in Tom's eyes and it looks to me as if there's a choked disk there. I would almost bet my life on it. I want to call in a good eye man, and I want to have another set of X rays taken the first thing tomorrow morning."[12]

Dr. Watts asked that Mabel have Annie Laurie Crawford, a young registered nurse who had befriended Wolfe and Mabel at Providence, accompany Wolfe the next day for the X rays. Miss Crawford had grown fond of Wolfe and had been helping as if she were his private nurse, spending hours of her off-duty time offering reassurance. Miss Crawford had been head nurse at Highland Hospital in Asheville and knew some of Wolfe's Westall cousins, and it was a comfort to Wolfe and Mabel to have someone from home nearby.

The next day Wolfe did not recognize Miss Crawford when she arrived to take him for X rays. After the X rays, Wolfe slept while the doctors broke the news to Mabel. The physicians believed Wolfe had an abscess or a tumor of the brain. They recommended he be taken to Johns Hopkins Hospital in Baltimore where the best brain surgeon in the country, Dr. Walter E. Dandy, could examine him. Dr. Watts suggested Mabel take Miss Crawford on the train to care for Wolfe and, if needed, give morphine injections for his headaches. He released Wolfe from Providence and allowed him one night in the Spring Hotel Apartments.

Wolfe, Mabel, and Miss Crawford left Seattle by rail on the *Olympian.* For four days Wolfe endured the trip across the continent, experiencing periods of irrationality and headaches. They changed trains at Chicago where Julia met them. Testing Wolfe's rationality, Mabel asked if he recognized the woman hurrying toward them on the platform. "Mrs. Julia E. Wolfe of the Old Kentucky Home!"[13] he greeted his mother and kissed her.

Arriving in Baltimore on September 10, the entourage was met by an ambulance sent by Johns Hopkins Hospital. Wolfe was drowsy when admitted to the hospital but tried to co-operate. Family members provided the data for his admission; he was too confused and ill to supply dependable information. Edward Aswell visited Wolfe in the hospital's Marburg Building and reassured him how wonderful his manuscript was. Aswell remembered: "And he began talking to me very lucidly, very clearly, and suddenly he stopped in the middle of a sentence, and it was as though a shade had been drawn on a scene you'd been looking at. The shade came down, everything went blank. He sat there for a moment, not looking around wildly or anything, just blank. The shade then went up. He resumed the sentence in the middle, exactly where it was." [14]

After Dr. Dandy examined Wolfe, he ushered Aswell, Julia, and Mabel into an empty room and told them, "I want to tell you about your son and brother. He's a desperately sick man. I doubt if there's a thing that can be done for him. I've just examined him—there's so much pressure in his head, it's hard as a rock. Now if it's cancer, the case is hopeless. And if it's multiple tuberculosis, it's hopeless—there's absolutely nothing we can do. There's only one chance: if it's an abscess or a tumor—and it depends a great deal on where it is—if it's right here," he pointed to the back of his head, "there may be some hope." Mabel asked what her brother's chances were. "They're ninety-five per cent against him," Dr. Dandy answered. "But if he had only one chance in a million, we ought to try to save him: he has that right." [15] Dr. Dandy recommended that trephining be performed to decrease pressure on Wolfe's brain—the pressure was so great it was bulging his eyes. Also, trephining would make it possible to put air in the brain for X-ray diagnosis.

The trephining procedure was performed that afternoon. When the right ventricle of Wolfe's brain was tapped, fluid spurted three feet. According to Dr. Dandy's medical report, "It was perfectly clear fluid, but contained 230 cells, 75% mononu-cleare. This was enough to make the diagnosis of tuberculosis." [16] For a short time, Wolfe's headaches were relieved. "They've fixed

it, Ed, they've fixed it,"[17] Wolfe told Aswell. But relief was tem-
porary. Dr. Dandy knew the only remaining hope was that
instead of many tubercles there might be only one, a tubercu-
loma, which could be removed.

Aswell returned to New York to break the news to Harper's;
and Elizabeth Nowell, Fred Wolfe, and Maxwell Perkins came to
the hospital. Aline Bernstein wanted to come but was dissuaded
by Perkins who knew Mrs. Bernstein's presence would disturb
Julia Wolfe. "Julia is here, and we don't know what she would do
if she sees you," Perkins told Mrs. Bernstein. "I really think it's
better for Tom if you don't come."[18]

The surgery was scheduled for September 12. Wolfe's family
and friends remained in a small waiting room near the operating
room. At the family's insistence, Annie Laurie Crawford watched
the operation and served as a buffer between hospital staff and
family. Dr. Dandy performed a cerebellar exploration, looking
for a large tubercle that might be causing the obstruction to the
flow of cerebrospinal fluid and therefore increasing the pressure.
If this could be found and removed, the pressure might be relieved. Unfortunately, during surgery, Dr. Dandy discovered
"Over the right lobe of the cerebellum were myriads of tubercles" and determined "Obviously there was nothing that could
be done."[19] The wound was closed with sutures of layered silk.

"He didn't operate," Annie Laurie Crawford told Wolfe's family and friends. "They opened up Tom's skull, and Dr. Dandy took
one look and laid the scalpel down."[20] Dr. Dandy then came into
the waiting room, still in his white suit and skullcap. "The case
is hopeless," he grimly told everyone. "He has miliary tuberculosis of the brain. His brain is simply covered with tubercles—
there must be millions of them there." The family exploded with
grief and shock. "He may live for six weeks more," Dr. Dandy
told them when they calmed down, "and we can keep him fairly
comfortable. But it's absolutely hopeless. If he can die now, without recovering from the operation—as he may within the next
three days—it will be much better."[21] Dr. Dandy diagnosed that

Wolfe had contracted tuberculosis of the lung at some time in his youth. The lung cured itself, sealing the tubercles inside. When he contracted pneumonia in July, the lesion had reopened and the tubercles suffused his bloodstream and infected his brain.

Wolfe remained in the neurosurgical recovery room and did not return to the room he had been admitted to in the Marburg Building. For three days and nights, he lay in a semicoma. Elizabeth Nowell later recalled: "His head was swathed in great white bandages, his eyes were shut, his breath came stertorously through half-opened mouth, but perhaps a spark of consciousness still was in him."[22] According to hospital records, Wolfe regained consciousness and talked with family members on September 13. The following day, lapsing into unconsciousness, he called for "Scotch!" and had imaginary conversations with his New York editors.

The nurses urged Mabel to try to communicate with her brother. "Tom!" she would cry out, "Tom! Can you hear me? Answer me! Tom! Tom!" Finally, Wolfe answered with infinite patience and weariness, as if already talking to her from another world: "All right, Mabel. I'm coming. . . ."[23]

A blood transfusion was given to him but to no avail. Wolfe died on Thursday morning, September 15, at 5:30. His death certificate lists the immediate cause of death as "tuberculosis meningitis" with contributing "pulmonary tuberculosis." However, pneumonia developed following the major surgery and, like his brother Ben, Wolfe died "drowning . . . in his own secretions."[24] He died so suddenly there was little time to call those who had waited so loyally near him. (Of Wolfe's family and friends, only Annie Laurie Crawford witnessed his death.) "At the end—the very end—nothing but silence—there will be silence, lonely silence in the end,"[25] he had written earlier. Julia, Mabel, and Fred arrived five minutes after Wolfe died. Beside himself with grief, Fred implored the doctors to do something: "Bring him back, for ten minutes, five minutes, one minute! I want to talk to him!" "You do not understand," Mabel told Fred. "Tom is dead."[26]

Julia Wolfe's face as she left the hospital was "white, almost like marble," her granddaughter Virginia remembered, "her black-brown eyes were frightened."[27] Julia did not sleep that night, but sat at a window in the rooming house across from Johns Hopkins, watching the hospital, refusing to go to bed. (Tom, she later insisted, had died of a brain abscess following pneumonia—tuberculosis was never mentioned.)

A coffin large enough to hold Wolfe's body could not be located in Baltimore, so the undertaker had one made to order. On September 16 the king-size coffin was loaded onto a baggage car before Wolfe's family boarded the train. Elizabeth Nowell and Edward Aswell noticed that the family Pullman car was K-19, the car Wolfe usually took to Asheville.

On Saturday morning, the 17th, the train climbed up through the hills and mountains Wolfe had loved so much and arrived at the Biltmore station at 9:15. His body was taken to the Brownell-Dunn Funeral Home directly across the street from the Old Kentucky Home where final touches were provided. After an hour, his remains were moved into the front parlor of the dilapidated house he had always hated. Surrounded by floral tributes, he lay rigid in the pink padded, satin-lined casket, rouged and embalmed, his face white and expressionless, the line of his mouth unnatural and set. His nicotine-stained hands were

Julia Wolfe, shortly before her death in 1945. Julia outlived Thomas Wolfe by seven years. Despite the fact that Wolfe's doctors diagnosed that he had contracted tuberculosis in his youth, Julia refused to admit that her son had died of the disease. Maxwell Perkins firmly believed that Wolfe had contracted tuberculosis in Julia's boardinghouse, where her mania for money made her careless about the boarders she accepted.

Photo courtesy of The Thomas Wolfe Collection, Pack Memorial Public Library, Asheville, North Carolina.

waxen, the callus on his finger tangible evidence that writing was indeed hard work. An ill-fitting black wig hid the incision on his shaved skull. The hair was plastered down, sleek and smooth, and shined like patent leather. Mabel placed a red rose in the lapel of his blue serge suit, although she knew her brother would not approve. The coffin, draped with transparent pink cheesecloth to keep the flies away, lay only a few feet from the piano where Mabel had entertained during the house's salad days.

News of Thomas Wolfe's death stunned the community. Hundreds of friends and admirers called that day. Julia stood by the coffin, tearless, incessantly describing every minute detail of her son's final illness to anyone who would listen. Mabel, reeking with whiskey, stood near Julia, contradicting her mother's stories, and often weeping into her handkerchief. Maxwell Perkins went in to look at Wolfe, "who, thank God, did not look in the least like Tom," Perkins later remembered, "so I didn't much mind what I had dreaded."[28] Frederick Koch, Wolfe's playwriting instructor at Chapel Hill, attempted to find violets for Wolfe. Koch remembered how Buck Gavin had gone searching for violets to put on the grave of his partner. For hours Koch scoured the city but could not locate the violets he thought so appropriate for his former student.

On Sunday afternoon, September 18, at 2:45, Thomas Wolfe left the Old Kentucky Home for the last time. The crowd gathered in front of the house overflowed from the yard to the sidewalk and street. As pallbearers J.Y. Jordan, Paul Green, Albert Coates, Frederick Koch, Jonathan Daniels, Hamilton Basso, W.O. Wolfe, Jr., and Henry Westall carried the coffin out of the parlor, Mabel began screaming hysterically. She later admitted she could not remember anything for the next two weeks. Pressed to the limits of her endurance, she did not attend her brother's funeral.[29]

"Brief, but impressive funeral services"[30] were held at First Presbyterian Church where Wolfe had attended Sunday school as a boy. The church was full a half-hour before the three o'clock services began, and the crowd extended to the church's balcony and lawn. Rev. Robert F. Campbell, the former pastor, officiated, assisted by the present pastor, Rev. C. Grier Davis. "Abide with Me" and "Crossing the Bar," hymns chosen by Mabel, were sung. Dr. Campbell told the assembly, "I wish I had something definite to say about his religious life. As there was a restlessness and lack of definite form in his intellectual and emotional processes, it is natural to conclude that the same was true of his religious beliefs and aspirations." Campbell illustrated his contention with a quotation from *Of Time and the River:* "Where shall the weary rest? When shall the lonely of heart come home? What doors are open for the wanderer? And which of us shall find his father, know his face, and in what place, and in what time, and in what land?"[31] But when atheist Margaret Roberts sensed Dr. Campbell was attempting to add religious connotation by capitalizing "his" and "father" with special emphasis, she wanted to say, "Not capitals! No capitals there!"[32] ("Father" and "His" were capitalized in the *Asheville Citizen's* reportage of the funeral.)

As the funeral cortege passed through the business district, people along the streets stopped and bowed their heads. Men took off their hats. Hundreds attended the interment at Riverside Cemetery. At the end of the rites, Julia Wolfe's tired face was seen pressed against the window of her limousine, and, as the car rolled away, she watched the grave as long as she could.

Thomas Wolfe's net estate was assessed at $10,305. Cash at the time of his death totaled $8,653. Royalties accrued on his books were estimated at $6,009. Deductions for administrative and funeral costs of $2,026 and debts of $2,331, incurred during his final illness, reduced the total. Wolfe's will named Maxwell Perkins as executor of the estate.

The fate of Wolfe's massive unfinished manuscript was then in the hands of Edward Aswell. Only a day after Wolfe's death, the *Asheville Citizen* reported that Wolfe's last manuscript would "continue the story of the Gant family began in 'Look Homeward, Angel.'"[33] Before Wolfe had left for Purdue, he determined that *The Web and the Rock* would require at least another year of work. Although many chapters had been completed, others remained in first or partial draft, and several had yet to be written. Some of the sections were still in Wolfe's handwritten scrawl—typists would have to guess at some of the penciled words. In addition, the protagonist of the book had as many as six different names. In some chapters, which often weaved between first and third person, the protagonist had several brothers and sisters, while in others, he was an only child.

After Wolfe's death, Aswell and Perkins realized that because the novel was ten times the size of the average novel, there would be a small reading public for anything of such proportions. Allowed to use only the two enormous bundles Wolfe gave him in May 1937, Aswell dealt with the problem by dividing the manuscript into two novels: *The Web and the Rock* and *You Can't Go Home Again*, and a collection of stories and fragments, *The Hills Beyond*. He standardized names, blended or omitted characters, and, to prevent lawsuits for libel or invasion of privacy, changed the names or altered the descriptions of minor characters. Although Aswell took liberties in reshaping and recasting dozens of passages, as well as writing the summary notes appearing in italics between the sections of each novel, by no means could he be considered the author of Wolfe's posthumous novels, as some critics have charged.

Maxwell Perkins and Edward Aswell were asked by Wolfe's family to supply a suitable epitaph for Wolfe's gravestone. Perkins chose a quotation from *Look Homeward, Angel*; Aswell, one from *The Web and the Rock*. Although only one quotation was to be on the stone, Wolfe's family could not decide which to use, so they used both:

"THE LAST VOYAGE, THE LONGEST, THE BEST."

LOOK HOMEWARD, ANGEL

"DEATH BENT TO TOUCH HIS CHOSEN SON WITH MERCY, LOVE AND PITY, AND PUT THE SEAL OF HONOR ON HIM WHEN HE DIED."

THE WEB AND THE ROCK

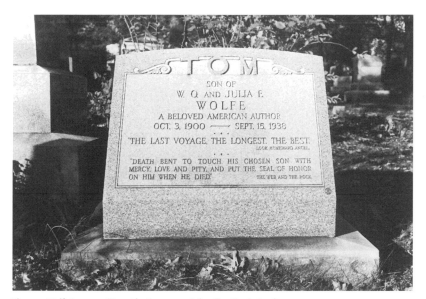

Thomas Wolfe's grave, Riverside Cemetery, Asheville, North Carolina.
Photo courtesy of The Thomas Wolfe Collection, Pack Memorial Public Library, Asheville, North Carolina.

NOTES

1. *Notebooks*, II, 954.

2. *Letters*, 764.

3. Thomas Wolfe, *You Can't Go Home Again* (New York: Harper & Brothers, 1940), 388.

4. *Letters*, 766.

5. *Notebooks*, II, 963.

6. *Ibid.*, 987.

7. *Letters*, 774.

8. *Ibid.*, 776.

9. Donald, 456.

10. *Letters*, 776.

11. Nowell, 428.

12. *Ibid.*, 429.

13. *Ibid.*, 434.

14. *Ibid.*, 436.

15. *Ibid.*

16. Medical reports, Johns Hopkins Hospital, September 10 and 12, 1938.

17. Nowell, 437.

18. Carole Klein. *Aline* (New York: Harper & Row, 1979), 316.

19. Medical reports.

20. Nowell, 438.

21. *Ibid.*

22. *Ibid.*

23. *Ibid.*, 438–439.

24. *The Autobiographical Outline*, 41.

25. *Notebooks*, II, 616.

26. *Charlotte News*, July 30, 1939.

27. Virginia Gambrell Wilder to Ted Mitchell, telephone interview, April 23, 1996.

28. Nowell, 439.

29. See Joanne Marshall Mauldin, "'Peace to His Ashes and Sorrow for His Going': Thomas Wolfe's Funeral," *Thomas Wolfe Review* 18:1 (Fall 1994): 31. This article is a definitive and fascinating account of Thomas Wolfe's funeral.

30. *Asheville Citizen*, September 19, 1938.

31. *Ibid.* In the early 1930s Wolfe claimed to be an atheist: "I do not think that I have believed in God for fifteen years. Sometimes it seems that I never believed in him save when I was a little child, saying my prayers, mechanically, at night." Turnbull, 327.

32. Turnbull, 321.

33. *Asheville Citizen*, September 16, 1938.

Carrara angel from the tombstone shop of W. O. Wolfe in Asheville. "It was sculpted from the finest white Italian marble that money could buy," Wolfe's father told the daughters of Margaret Bates Johnson, who purchased the statue for their mother's grave in 1906. The statue stands in Oakdale Cemetery, Hendersonville, North Carolina.

Photo by Ted Mitchell.

Thomas Wolfe's funeral, September 18, 1938, First Presbyterian church, Asheville.

Photo courtesy of the Thomas Wolfe Collection, Pack Memorial Public Library, Asheville, North Carolina.

Ancestry of Thomas Wolfe

Paternal Ancestry

Nothing has been learned of the parentage of Thomas Wolfe's paternal grandfather, Jacob Wolf. He may have been descended from or in some way related to Hans Georg Wolff or Hans Bernhard Wolff, immigrants who arrived in America in 1727. He may have been a distant cousin of George Wolf, governor (1829–1835) of Pennsylvania. Thomas Wolfe's paternal grandmother, Eleanor Jane Heikes, was of Dutch and German ancestry.

I.   Jacob Wolf was born about 1807 in Adams County, Pennsylvania; he died 17 August 1860. Married on 12 April 1838 to Eleanor Jane Heikes (13 July 1817–26 July 1913). They had nine children:

1. Augusta Louisa Wolf (1838–ca. 1915).
2. George Alexander Wolf (1839–1901).
3. Sarah Ellen Wolf (1841–1864).
4. Huldah Emeline Wolf (1844–1858).
5. Susan Rebecca Wolf (1846–1867).
6. Wesley Emerson Wolfe (1848–1915).
7. WILLIAM OLIVER WOLFE (Thomas Wolfe's father. See below.)
8. Elmore Elsworth (or Elmer Emerson) Wolf (1853–1894).
9. Gilbert John (or John Gilbert) Wolf (1858–1921).

II. William Oliver Wolfe (10 April 1851–20 June 1922). Married three times: Hattie J. Watson on 9 October 1873; Cynthia C.

Hill (1842–1884) on 25 March 1879; Julia Westall (16 February 1860–7 December 1945) on 14 January 1885. No children from W.O.'s first two marriages; eight children with Julia Westall Wolfe:

1. Leslie E. Wolfe (19 October 1885–14 July 1886).

2. Effie Nelson Wolfe Gambrell (7 June 1887–11 November 1950).

3. Frank Cecil Wolfe (25 November 1888–7 November 1956).

4. Mabel Elizabeth Wolfe Wheaton (25 September 1890–29 September 1958).

5. Benjamin Harrison Wolfe (27 October 1892–19 October 1918).

6. Grover Cleveland Wolfe (27 October 1892–16 November 1904).

7. Frederick William Wolfe (15 July 1894–8 April 1980).

8. Thomas Clayton Wolfe (3 October 1900–15 September 1938).

Maternal Ancestry

I. Richard (or Andrew) Westall. Origins England or Scotland.

II. Thomas Westall (sometimes referred to as William McGillis Westall), born in England or Scotland, about 1775; died circa 1834. Married Mary Brittain Westall (20 July 1787–27 November 1864) about 1804 (divorced in about 1812). One son.

III. William Brittain ("Billy") Westall (15 November 1805–22 November 1882). Married Matilda Penland Westall (30 June 1799–21 June 1841) on May 31, 1827. Six children from this marriage:

1. Samuel James Westall (1828–1897).

2. Thomas Casey Westall (1830–1903).

3. Clarissa Ann Westall Horton (1832–1921).
4. William Lysander Westall (1836–1864).
5. Noble Bachus Westall (1838–1924).
6. Matilda Jane Westall (1841, died shortly after birth).

William Brittain Westall's second marriage in 1841 was to Eliza Madelyn Angel (20 April 1820–19 November 1898) in 1841. There were 13 children from the second marriage:

1. John Baird Westall (1842–1937).
2. Henry Clay Westall (1843–1845).
3. Julia Catharine Westall (1845–1846).
4. Andrew Henson Westall (1846–1914).
5. Mary Elizabeth Westall (1848–?).
6. William Lysander Westall, born Winfield Scott Westall (1849– ca. 1876).
7. Rebecca Katie Westall (1850–?).
8. Robert Penland Westall (1853–1874).
9. James Poteat Westall (1854–1915).
10. Theodore Westall (1856–1925).
11. Sarah Ann Eliza Westall (1857–1911).
12. Zebulon Vance Westall (1859–1890).
13. Nancy Louisa Westall (1859–1953).

IV. Thomas Casey Westall (9 May 1830–28 June 1903). Married Martha Ann Penland Westall (31 March 1833–27 July 1899) on 31 January 1853. Eleven children:

1. Henry Addison Westall (1854–1947).
2. Samuel William Bacchus Westall (1855–1863).
3. Sarah Matilda Westall (1857–1877).
4. JULIA ELIZABETH WESTALL (1860–1945). (Thomas Wolfe's mother.)

5. James Manassas Westall (1861–1943).
6. William Harrison Westall (1863–1944).
7. Lee Johnson Westall (1866–1884).
8. Mary Rebecca Westall (1868–1885).
9. Thomas Crockett Westall (1870–1940).
10. Horace Greely Westall (1872–1902).
11. Elmer Capen Westall (1874–1941).

(Sources: *Julia and the Westalls Beyond: The Maternal Ancestry of Thomas Wolfe,* Deborah A. Borland, 1992; *Thomas Wolfe's Pennsylvania,* Richard Walser, Croissant & Company, 1978; "Thomas Westall and His Son William," Richard Walser, *Thomas Wolfe Review,* (Spring 1984,): 8–18.)

Thomas Wolfe's great-half-uncle, John B. Westall (1842–1937), as a Confederate soldier. Wolfe fictionalized his uncle's reminiscences of the Civil War battle at Chickamauga into a short story, "Chickamauga." However, in the story, Westall was made more countrified. "Grandfather didn't talk the way the speaker does in the story, though," Westall's grandson, Bruce Westall, later remembered. "He was very precise and careful; he never said 'hit' for 'it.'" (*Thomas Wolfe Review,* Fall 1982.)

Photo courtesy of The North Carolina Collection, Pack Memorial Public Library, Asheville, North Carolina.

Publications of Thomas Wolfe

Separate Publications

The Crisis in Industry, University of North Carolina, 1919.

Look Homeward, Angel, Charles Scribner's Sons, 1929.

Of Time and the River, Charles Scribner's Sons, 1935.

From Death to Morning, Charles Scribner's Sons, 1935.

The Story of a Novel, Charles Scribner's Sons, 1936.

A Note on Experts: Dexter Vespasian Joyner, House of Books, Ltd., 1939.

The Web and the Rock, Harper & Brothers, 1939.

You Can't Go Home Again, Harper & Brothers, 1940.

The Hills Beyond, Harper & Brothers, 1941.

Gentlemen of the Press, Black Archer Press, 1942.

Thomas Wolfe's Letters to His Mother, Charles Scribner's Sons, 1943.

Mannerhouse, Harper & Brothers, 1948.

. . . *"The Years of Wandering in Many Lands and Cities,"* Charles S. Boesen, 1949.

A Western Journal, University of Pittsburgh Press, 1951.

The Correspondence of Thomas Wolfe and Homer Andrew Watt, New York University Press, 1954.

The Letters of Thomas Wolfe, Charles Scribner's Sons, 1956.

The Short Novels of Thomas Wolfe, Charles Scribner's Sons, 1961.

Thomas Wolfe's Purdue Speech: "Writing and Living," Purdue University Studies, 1964.

The Mountains, University of North Carolina Press, 1970.

The Notebooks of Thomas Wolfe, University of North Carolina Press, 1970.

A Prologue to America, Croissant & Company, 1978.

London Tower, Thomas Wolfe Society, 1980.

The Proem to "O Lost," Thomas Wolfe Society, 1980.

The Streets of Durham, Thomas Wolfe Society, 1982.

K-19: Salvaged Pieces, Thomas Wolfe Society, 1983.

Welcome to Our City, Louisiana State University Press, 1983.

Beyond Love and Loyalty: The Letters of Thomas Wolfe and Elizabeth Nowell, University of North Carolina Press, 1983.

My Other Loneliness: Letters of Thomas Wolfe and Aline Bernstein, University of North Carolina Press, 1983.

The Train and the City, Thomas Wolfe Society, 1984.

Holding on for Heaven: The Cables and Postcards of Thomas Wolfe and Aline Bernstein, Thomas Wolfe Society, 1985.

Thomas Wolfe Interviewed, 1929–1938, Louisiana State University Press, 1985.

The Hound of Darkness, Thomas Wolfe Society, 1986.

The Complete Short Stories of Thomas Wolfe, Charles Scribner's Sons, 1987.

The Starwick Episodes, Thomas Wolfe Society, 1989.

Thomas Wolfe's Composition Books: The North State Fitting School 1912–1915, Thomas Wolfe Society, 1990.

The Autobiographical Outline for Look Homeward, Angel, Thomas Wolfe Society, 1991.

The Good Child's River, University of North Carolina Press, 1991.

The Lost Boy, University of North Carolina Press, 1992.

Thomas Wolfe's Notes on Macbeth, Thomas Wolfe Society, 1992.

[George Webber, Writer]: An Introduction by a Friend, Thomas Wolfe Society, 1994.

The Party at Jack's, University of North Carolina Press, 1995.

Antaeus, or A Memory of Earth, Thomas Wolfe Society, 1996.

Passage to England: A Selection, Thomas Wolfe Society, 1998.

First-Appearance Contributions to Books, Magazines, and Newspapers

"A Field in Flanders," *University of North Carolina Magazine*, December 1917.

"To France," *University of North Carolina Magazine*, December 1917.

"The Challenge," *University of North Carolina Magazine*, March 1918.

"A Cullenden of Virginia," *University of North Carolina Magazine*, March 1918.

"To Rupert Brooke," *University of North Carolina Magazine*, May 1918.

"The Drammer," *University of North Carolina Magazine*, April 1919.

"An Appreciation," *University of North Carolina Magazine*, May 1919.

"Deferred Payment," *University of North Carolina Magazine*, June 1919.

"Russian Folk Song," *University of North Carolina Magazine*, May 1920.

"The Creative Movement in Writing," *Tar Heel*, June 14, 1919.

"The Streets of Durham, or Dirty Work at the Cross Roads," *University of North Carolina Tar Baby*, November 18, 1919.

"Concerning Honest Bob," *University of North Carolina Magazine*, May 1920.

"The Return of Buck Gavin," *Carolina Folk-Plays*, Henry Holt & Company, 1924.

"London Tower," *Asheville Citizen*, July 19, 1925.

"An Angel on the Porch," *Scribner's Magazine*, August 1929.

"A Poetic Odyssey of the Korea That Was Crushed," *New York Evening Post*, April 4, 1931.

"A Portrait of Bascom Hawke," *Scribner's Magazine*, April 1932.

"The Web of Earth," *Scribner's Magazine*, July 1932.

"The Train and the City," *Scribner's Magazine*, May 1933.

"Death the Proud Brother," *Scribner's Magazine*, June 1933.

"No Door: A Story of Time and the Wanderer," *Scribner's Magazine*, July 1933.

"The Four Lost Men," *Scribner's Magazine*, February 1934.

"The Sun and the Rain," *Scribner's Magazine*, May 1934.

"Boom Town," *American Mercury*, May 1934.

"The House of the Far and Lost," *Scribner's Magazine*, August 1934.

"Dark in the Forest, Strange as Time," *Scribner's Magazine*, November 1934.

"The Names of the Nation," *Modern Monthly*, December 1934.

"For Professional Appearance," *Modern Monthly*, January 1935.

"One of the Girls in Our Party," *Scribner's Magazine*, January 1935.

"Circus at Dawn," *Modern Monthly*, March 1935.

"His Father's Earth," *Modern Monthly*, April 1935.

"Old Catawba," *Virginia Quarterly Review*, April 1935.

"Only the Dead Know Brooklyn," *New Yorker*, June 15, 1935.

"Polyphemus," *North American Review*, June 1935.

"In the Park," *Harper's Bazaar*, June 1935.

"The Face of the War," *Modern Monthly*, June 1935.

"Gulliver: The Story of a Tall Man," *Scribner's Magazine*, June 1935.

"Arnold Pentland," *Esquire*, June 1935.

"Cottage by the Tracks," *Cosmopolitan*, July 1935.

"The Bums at Sunset," *Vanity Fair*, October 1935.

"The Bell Remembered," *American Mercury*, August 1936.

"Fame and the Poet," *American Mercury*, October 1936.

"I Have a Thing to Tell You: (Nun will ich ihnen 'was sagen)." *New Republic*, March 10, 17, 24, 1937.

"Mr. Malone," *New Yorker*, May 29, 1937.

"Oktoberfest," *Scribner's Magazine*, June 1937.

"'E, A Recollection," *New Yorker*, July 17, 1937.

"April, Late April," *American Mercury*, September 1937.

"The Child by Tiger," *Saturday Evening Post*, September 11, 1937.

"Katamoto," *Harper's Bazaar*, October 1937.

"The Lost Boy," *Redbook*, November 1937.

"Chickamauga," *Yale Review*, Winter 1938.

"The Company," *New Masses*, January 11, 1938.

"A Prologue to America," *Vogue*, February 1, 1938.

The Third Night: A Play of the Carolina Mountains, *The Carolina Playbook*, September 11, 1938.

"Portrait of a Literary Critic: A Satire," *American Mercury*, April 1939.

"The Party at Jack's," *Scribner's Magazine*, May 1939.

"A Western Journey," *Virginia Quarterly Review*, Summer 1939.

"Three O'Clock," *North American Review*, Summer 1939.

"The Winter of Our Discontent," *Atlantic Monthly*, June 1939.

"The Golden City," *Harper's Bazaar*, June 1939.

"The Birthday," *Harper's Magazine*, June 1939.

"Enchanted City," *Reader's Digest*, October 1939.

"The Hollyhock Sowers," *American Mercury*, August 1940.

"Dark Messiah," *Current History and Forum*, August 1940.

"Nebraska Crane," *Harper's Magazine*, August 1940.

"So This Is Man," *Town and Country*, August 1940.

"The Promise of America," *Coronet*, September 1940.

"The Hollow Men," *Esquire*, October 1940.

"The Anatomy of Loneliness," *American Mercury*, October 1941.

"The Lion at Morning," *Harper's Bazaar*, October 1941.

"The Plumed Knight," *Town and Country*, October 1941.

"Old Man Rivers," *Atlantic Monthly*, December 1947.

(Sources: *Thomas Wolfe: A Descriptive Bibliography*, Carol Johnston, University of Pittsburgh Press, 1987; "Thomas Wolfe: A Publishing Chronology," Aldo P. Magi, *Thomas Wolfe Review* (Fall 1983):14–20.)

Acknowledgments

FOREMOST, I express my gratitude to Steve Hill, manager of the Thomas Wolfe Memorial since 1979, who made this book a reality. Without his idea for a concise Thomas Wolfe biography, this book would not have been written.

As always, I am indebted to Aldo P. Magi for his extraordinary kindness. He is an outstanding advisor and friend, and I deeply appreciate his generosity of spirit and his constant willingness to assist. That's why this book is dedicated to him.

Dr. Richard Knapp's sound counsel guided the manuscript from its first stages to the final draft. His efficient and generous help improved this book by 100 percent. I cannot thank him enough for his advice.

I am especially indebted to Philip P. Banks of Pack Memorial Public Library, Asheville. He was always eager to help me locate materials from numerous sources. I am also grateful to the staff of the Houghton Library at Harvard University, especially Leslie Morris and Melanie Wisner. I am grateful to Alice R. Cotten and Jerry Cotten at the Wilson Library, University of North Carolina at Chapel Hill, for their attention to minute details.

David Strange provided the design and composition of the first edition, upon which this revision is based. As always, I am grateful for his advice as a counselor and his remarkable talents as a designer. His enormous generosity of time and talent will always be appreciated.

I am grateful to the following individuals for answering my questions and sharing their knowledge of Thomas Wolfe: James W. Clark, Jr., Walter E. Dandy, Jr., M.D., Mary Aswell Doll, Elizabeth Evans, Richard S. Kennedy, John L. Idol, Jr., Steven B. Rogers, Webb Salmon, Herbert M. Schiller, M.D., Clara Stites, Morton I. Teicher, and John Ware, M.D.

Many thanks to Deborah A. Borland, whose expertise and professionalism assisted so greatly in the preparation of this book.

I am especially grateful to Tim Barnwell, John Beaver, the late Paul Gitlin, Kimberley Hewitt, Joe A. Mobley, Chris Morton, Zoe Rhine, Susan Weatherford, Ralph Williams, and Ann Wright, for their assistance.

I would also like to thank for their support: my parents, Ilias and Edna Mitchell; my brother, Rick Mitchell and his family; and friends Zeb Baker, Connie Bostic, Matthew J. Bruccoli, Pat Conroy, George Darden, Tina Gambrell, Walter R. Graham, Jr., Allan Gurganus, Jan Hensley, Secretary Betty Ray McCain, Wes Morrison, Henry Rollins, Anne W. Taylor, Chris Wexler, and the late Virginia Wilder. My Sunday afternoon visits with the late Margaret Rose Roberts contained some of the most moving memories of my life.

My greatest debt, however, is to Joanne Marshall Mauldin, certainly one of the finest Wolfe researchers in the country. Not only have her painstakingly researched articles set an example for Wolfe scholarship to come, but her fierce devotion to maintaining accuracy and clarity has been an inspiration to me. Without Joanne Mauldin's help, this would have been a different volume altogether.

* * * * *

Finally, Todd Bailey has proved to be all that a friend can be. Life is lighter with his presence.

LEE COUNTY LIBRARY
107 Hawkin
Sanford.

INDEX